JOURNEY TO WEALTH

WEALTH IS FUNDAMENTALLY A PERSONAL CHOICE

BY: JOSHUA GREAT

All rights reserved. The unauthorized reproduction or distribution of this copyrighted work is illegal. No part of this book may be used or reproduced electronically or in print without written permission by the author.

Copyright © 2017, JOSHUA GREAT
Project Manager: Campaign Coachsulting Strategist Dr. Serena Washington
Cover Artist: Second Covenant Mogul Publishing

The material in this book is confidential, privileged or constitutes work product, and is intended only for the use of JOSHUA GREAT named above. If you are not the intended recipient, be advised that unauthorized use, disclosure, copying, distribution, or the taking of any action in reliance on this information is strictly prohibited. All knowledge is held by JOSHUA GREAT and no one else is authorized to speak on events in this book, because I JOSHUA GREAT hold all rights and copy rights. If you are an Thank you for respecting my works written to bring awareness to the world.

DEDICATION

This great book is dedicated to GOD ALMIGHTY without whom this book would not have been possible.

To my lovely wife PRAISE whose support, love and commitment has made this book possible. When all hope was gone, she stood strong and went the extra mile. There is nothing I can give to her that will really make up for all she has done and is still doing. God bless you, my dear wife.

To my beautiful children, Olivia, Shepherd and Divine. Their fervent prayers and desire to see daddy succeed is truly amazing. I love you all. God bless you all.

JOURNEY TO WEALTH

CONTENTS

CHAPTER 1 - BEYOND THIS 6

CHAPTER 2 - THE CORE 40

CHAPTER 3 - YOU HAVE IT 63

CHAPTER 4 - IT IS NOT NATURAL ...77

CHAPTER 5 - TAP INTO IT 83

CHAPTER 6 - YOUR WELLS 115

CHAPTER 7 - THE STROKE 135

CHAPTER 8 - THE FACTOR 165

JOURNEY TO WEALTH

WEALTH IS FUNDAMENTALLY A PERSONAL CHOICE

BY: JOSHUA GREAT

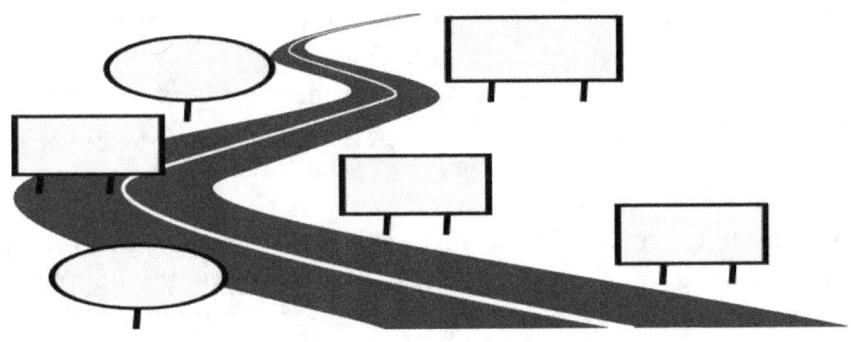

JOURNEY TO WEALTH.

CHAPTER ONE
BEYOND THIS

A long time ago, there was a very grievous famine over every land except Egypt. There was no food anywhere except Egypt. And as expected, everyone, every nation including Israel marched to Egypt for survival. As the children of Israel moved towards Egypt along with people from other parts of the world, survival became the driving force.

Survival became everyone's quest. Even the Egyptians were not spared from the famine. Even though there was food in Egypt, the Egyptians still had to join the rest of the world in buying food in Egypt for themselves. The food in Egypt was not collective or general.

The food in Egypt was political. The food in Egypt was not for everyone. The food in Egypt was stored in the name of Pharaoh under the leadership care of Joseph. As such, even the Egyptians had to buy food from their country Egypt just like every other person so that they could survive.

Everyone moved from every part of the world to get food from Egypt so that they could survive. As they moved, Egypt emerged as the wealthiest country in the world. Everyone came with their money, their substance and their treasures to Egypt and this made Egypt the wealthiest nation in the world.

"And all countries came into Egypt to Joseph for to buy corn; because that the famine was so sore in all lands." – Genesis 41:57.

Every money currency in the world was submitted to Egypt. Wealth flowed like great rivers to Egypt. While every other person and country were struggling to survive, and giving out their money to buy food from Egypt; Egypt on the other hand stood above survival and was growing in great dimensions of wealth. Wealth ran parallel to survival. It was wealth against survival.

Everyone who came to Egypt for food, came with their money to buy food. No one came to Egypt to tell stories. Everyone who came for food, came prepared. If there was any other alternative apart from Egypt, a lot of people would have towed the line of that alternative. But there was no other alternative. Egypt was everyone's only alternative.

NO OTHER CHOICE

Egypt was the only choice everyone had. Whether people liked Egypt or not; if they must survive then they must go to Egypt. Everyone out of their desperate need to survive, trooped down to Egypt for food, they released their money to Egypt.

In exchange for food, people released their wealth and possessions for food all in a bid to survive. The rich could not eat their wealth and possessions as there was no food anywhere apart from Egypt. Everyone had to exchange their wealth and possessions for food so that they could survive.

Survival is the single most important basic need of everyone. Everyone primarily has to survive. As people in their quest to survive trooped down to Egypt, everything they had went for food. Survival drained the people and was gradually reducing everyone to poverty.

THE NEED TO SURVIVE

But Egypt was not bothered about surviving because she had abundance, As everyone was getting poorer by the day in their earnest bid to survive, Egypt was getting richer by the day. Soon everyone exhausted all they had. Survival drove people to poverty.

It even got so bad that when there was no money, people started selling themselves to survive. The wealthy now became poor and the poor became poorer, all because of the need to survive.

"And there was no bread in all the land;
for the famine was very sore,
so that the land of Egypt and all the land of Canaan

fainted by reason of the famine.

*And Joseph gathered up all the
money that was found in the land of Egypt,
and in the land of Canaan,
for the corn which they bought,
and Joseph brought the money into Pharaoh's house.*

*And when money failed
in the land of Egypt, and in the
land of Canaan, all the Egyptians came unto Joseph,
and said, Give us bread:
for why should we die in thy presence?
For the money faileth.*

*And Joseph said, give your cattle,
and I will give you for your cattle, if money fail.*

*And they brought their cattle unto Joseph:
and Joseph gave them bread for horses,
and for flocks, and for cattle of the herds,
and for the asses, and he fed them with bread
for all their cattle for that year.*

*When that year was ended,
they came unto him the second year,
and said, we will not hide it from my lord,
my lord also had our herd of cattle,
there is not aught left in the sight of my lord,
but our bodies, and our lands.*

*Wherefore shall we die before thine eyes,
both we and our land?
Buy us and our land for bread,
and we and our land shall be the
servants unto Pharaoh: and give us seed,
that we may live and not die,
that the land be not desolate.*

> *And Joseph bought all the land*
> *of Egypt for Pharaoh: for the Egyptians*
> *sold everyman his field, because*
> *the famine prevailed over them:*
> *so the land became Pharaoh's."*
>
> *– Genesis 47:13-20.*

Everyone including the wealthy sold their lands, their possessions, and their bodies so that they could survive. No one had anything anymore. Everyone was stripped of all they had so that they could survive. And yet Egypt under the able leadership of Joseph lived in super abundance.

YOU MUST BEAT IT

Nothing drains people like the need to survive. Your journey to wealth begins with overcoming survival. Staying above survival is what marks the beginning of your journey to wealth. Overcoming survival is what qualifies you for wealth. Nothing fundamentally qualifies you for wealth like your victory over survival.

Until your concern for survival is over, you cannot access wealth. As long as you are still struggling to survive, you have not started your journey to wealth. Survival is the difference between the wealthy and the poor. Survival is what separates the wealthy from the poor.

While the wealthy have overcome survival, the poor are still struggling to survive. While the wealthy are not concerned about survival, the poor have survival as their major and ultimate concern. Wealth might be everyone's desire but wealth will not be everyone's reality. It is not everyone who will be wealthy.

While wealth is generally desirable, wealth is only exclusively accessible- exclusive in a selective sense and manner. Until you overcome survival, you cannot experience wealth. Survival is your major hindrance to wealth. Survival is your first challenge to wealth.

GO BEYOND SURVIVAL

As long as you are still struggling to put body and soul together, you have not started your journey to wealth. As long as you are still struggling to pay bills, your journey has not begun. You only begin your journey to wealth when survival is clearly out of the picture. You need to overcome the miserable scourge of survival if you must become wealthy.

You need to defeat survival in its entirety if you must enjoy wealth. Everyone in the days of Joseph was reduced to poverty by survival. Survival drives men to poverty. Survival drives men to lack. Anyone driven by survival cannot arrive at wealth.

At the root of poverty is survival. Survival is the character of poverty. Survival is the nature of poverty. Survival is the soul of poverty. Survival is the proof of poverty.

THE KEY

The first step to conquer poverty is to conquer survival. Survival is the clearest definition of poverty. As such, poverty is contending with survival. Poverty is battling with survival. The poor sleeps and wakes up thinking about how to survive. Survival is the thought of the poor. Survival is the heartbeat of the poor. Survival is the force behind poverty.

One of the poorest men in the whole of the scriptures was a man named Lazarus. Lazarus was in every bit and inch very poor. Everything about Lazarus oozed with poverty. Lazarus was a personification of poverty.

> *"There was a certain rich man,*
> *which was clothed in purple and fine linen,*
> *and fared sumptuously everyday:*
>
> *And there was a certain*
> *beggar named Lazarus,*
> *which was laid at his gate, full of sores.*
>
> *And desiring to be fed with the*
> *crumbs which fell from the rich man's table:*
> *moreover the dogs came and licked his sores."*

– Luke 16:19-21.

Everyday Lazarus sat at the gate of the rich man to beg for food and the reason Lazarus begged was so that he could survive. Where ever you see poverty, you see survival. Poverty and survival are two sides of the same dismal coin. **Poverty is bad. Poverty is evil. Poverty is dangerous.**

Poverty places people at the mercy of people. Poverty robs people of their choices and dignity. This is why you need to overcome poverty. This is why you need to come out of poverty and coming out of poverty lies in overcoming survival. Your battle against poverty is your battle against survival.

HOW YOU CAN OVERCOME SURVIVAL AND THEREBY BEGIN YOUR JOURNEY TO WEALTH.

PREPARATION

When Pharaoh had the dreams that revealed the coming global famine, Pharaoh did not know what those dreams meant. All the wise men of Egypt tried in futility to interpret Pharaoh's dreams. But when Joseph came, he interpreted Pharaoh's dreams with ease as an indication of a coming global affliction.

> *"And Joseph said unto Pharaoh,*
> *the dream of Pharaoh is one;*
> *God hath shown Pharaoh what he is about to do.*
>
> *The seven good kine are seven years;*
> *and the seven good ears are seven years;*
> *the dream is one.*
>
> *And the seven thin and ill favored kine*
> *that came up after them are seven years;*
> *and the seven empty ears blasted with*
> *the east wind shall be seven years of famine.*

*This is the thing which
I have spoken unto Pharaoh:
what God is about to do he showeth to Pharaoh.*

*Behold, there come seven years of
great plenty through out all the land of Egypt:*

*And there shall arise after
them seven years of famine:
and all the plenty shall be
forgotten in the land of Egypt:
and the famine shall consume the land;*

*And the plenty shall not be known
in the land by reason of the famine following:
for it shall be very grievous.*

*And for that the dream was
doubled unto Pharaoh twice,
it is because the thing is established by God,
and God will shortly bring it to pass."*

– Genesis 41:25-32.

As soon as Joseph interpreted Pharaoh's dreams, Joseph immediately counseled Pharaoh to begin preparations to tackle the coming global famine.

*"Now therefore let
Pharaoh look out a man,
discreet and wise,
and set him over the land of Egypt.*

*Let Pharaoh do this,
and let him appoint officers over the land,
and take up the fifth part of the
land of Egypt in the seven plenteous years.*

*And let them gather all the food
of those good years that come,
and lay up corn under the hand of Pharaoh,
and let them keep food in the cities.*

*And that food shall be for store to the
land against the seven years of famine,
which shall be in the land of Egypt;
that the land perish not through the famine."*

– *Genesis 41:33-36.*

Immediately after the interpretation was done, preparations began. Immediately after it came to the fore that for sure there was going to be a famine on a global scale, preparations took off. Things were put in place to checkmate the coming famine. And so, while everybody was struggling to survive because of the famine, Egypt escaped the lash of survival in the same famine by their deliberate preparations.

Instead of struggling for survival like every other person, Egypt lived in super abundance, far above survival; all because of their deliberate preparations. The famine that came was not selective. It was global. Everyone was expected to suffer from the famine but Egypt was exempted. Egypt escaped the scourge of the deadly famine because of her calculated preparations.

ESCAPE THE STRUGGLE

The reason why so many are struggling to survive is because many lack the necessary personal preparations to stay above survival. Even though so many may hate poverty, yet, so many are not prepared to come out of poverty. Many are not prepared to beat survival. You need preparations to come out of poverty. If you don't prepare, you will not get there.

A lot of people fail to prepare especially financially and that is why a lot of people struggle to survive. Egypt, under the able leadership of Joseph, had to prepare so that they could escape the famine and not get caught up by its whip. They had to prepare so that they will not become victims like others. It takes preparation to emerge victoriously. It takes preparation to escape being a victim.

It takes preparation to escape survival. It takes preparation to escape poverty. Poverty bows to deliberate preparation. Survival submits to thoughtful preparation. Your preparation is what empowers you to live above survival. Your preparation is what places you above poverty.

WEALTH GOES BEYOND LUCK

Nothing happens by chance. Nothing happens by luck. Anything that happens by chance does not stand a chance. You don't get wealthy by chance. You don't get wealthy by luck. Wealth is like someone with a destination. Wealth is like someone deliberately going somewhere. You must deliberately set yourself on the path to wealth and your preparation is what deliberately puts you on the path to wealth.

Wealth is essentially a product of careful, deliberate and calculated preparations. It takes great preparation to access wealth. Wealth is not an offspring of circumstance as many would want to believe; thinking that the rich are lucky or specially favoured. On the contrary, wealth is a product of deliberate preparations.

BE SMART ABOUT LIFE

Wealth requires preparations. Your wealth answers to your preparations. Men of wealth are men of great preparations. As you give yourself to preparations, survival becomes a thing of the past. No survival can withstand adequate preparations.

You don't wish away survival. You prepare against survival. Wherever you see people struggling to survive, you see people who lack the necessary preparations to beat survival. The wealthy don't get wealthy because they work harder or are essentially lucky. No! To think that way will be to have a faulty mentality. The wealthy are wealthy because they are smart and disciplined enough to put certain things in place that commands wealth.

Putting certain things in place is what preparation is all about. The difference between Egypt and the rest of the world was preparation. What separated Egypt from the rest of the world was preparation. What made

Egypt the focus of the world was preparation; years of careful and deliberate preparations channeled through lots of efforts and personal discipline.

MAKE A DIFFERENCE

Before the famine, there was nothing so special about Egypt. Egypt was like any other country. But when the famine came, Egypt suddenly became so special. Egypt became so important. Egypt became an imperative focus. To ignore Egypt as at that time would only be to your peril and menace.

Egypt became the compulsory destination of the world. If Egypt had not prepared, Egypt would have ended up as a victim, trying to survive like the rest of the world. But Egypt was not like the rest of the world. Egypt stood separated from the world. **Preparation makes you special.**

Preparation makes you different from others. Preparation makes you the focus of people. Preparation separates you from others. Preparation makes you the desire of people. The fundamental difference between the rich and the poor is preparation.

The core difference between wealth and poverty is preparation. The basal difference between success and failure is preparation. Preparation is the dividing line between wealth and poverty. Preparation is what separates wealth from poverty. Preparation is the nature of wealth.

PREPARE WITH THIS

Before the famine, there was food everywhere. No one was looking for food. Every country had food. No one knew that famine was coming except Egypt. It was only Egypt who had the privilege of knowing beforehand that there was going to be a global famine.

It was only Egypt who knew that there was going to be a global lack of food. If other countries had known, other countries would have prepared. But they did not know and the fact that they did not know was their peril and undoing.

The coming global famine was a privileged knowledge; privileged only to Egypt. And it was this privileged knowledge that moved Egypt to begin preparations. Egypt's preparation was a core function of her privileged knowledge. Egypt's preparation was driven by her privileged knowledge.

GO FOR KNOWLEDGE

Nothing determines preparations like knowledge. Nothing drives people to prepare like knowledge. Knowledge is the foundation of all preparation. Knowledge is the force behind every preparation. Preparation is a product of knowledge. Preparation does not just happen. Preparation is initiated by your deliberate pursuit of knowledge.

It takes knowledge to make preparations. Knowledge is what gives birth to preparation. Knowledge is what makes room for preparation. And so, preparation is knowledge at work. The only way to get prepared is to get knowledge. Those who lack preparation lack knowledge. Wherever preparation is lacking, knowledge is lacking. Until you begin to pursue knowledge, you will never know how to prepare.

THE THIRST DIMENSION

You don't just prepare because you want to prepare. Knowledge is what teaches you how to prepare. Knowledge shows you how to prepare. In order to prepare and overcome survival, you must seek out knowledge. Adequate preparation lies in the pursuit of adequate knowledge. You need to desire knowledge. You need to pursue knowledge. You need to give yourself to knowledge.

> ***"For I will pour water upon
> him that is thirsty,
> and floods upon the dry ground."***
>
> *-Isaiah 44:3.*

Only the thirsty qualify for water. Your thirst is your qualification for water. Without your thirst, you cannot access water. Water flows in the direction of thirst. Water answers to thirst. You must be thirsty if you must have water. Only those who thirst after knowledge, ever get knowledge. Knowledge does not flow to everyone.

Knowledge only flows to those who are thirsty. The door of knowledge is only opened to those who are thirsty for knowledge. Your thirst is the key. Knowledge is not by force. Knowledge is by thirst. Knowledge is by choice. Anyone who is thirsty, does not just sit and wish for water-that is not wisdom. To wish for knowledge is not wisdom. Knowledge goes beyond wishing.

GO FOR IT

Anyone who is truly thirsty goes out to look for water. Becoming thirsty, puts you on a compulsory pursuit for water. You don't wish for knowledge, you pursue knowledge. Knowledge is not wished for; knowledge is sought for. You must seek out knowledge if you must get knowledge.

Knowledge is not assumed. Knowledge is pursued. You can't be thirsty for knowledge and not go after knowledge. Your pursuit is what shows your thirst. Your pursuit is what proves your thirst. This is why pursuit is the proof of thirst. Pursuit is the proof of desire. Your thirst for knowledge is what puts you on the pursuit for knowledge.

Just as water answers to the pursuit of a thirsty man, in like manner, knowledge answers to the diligent pursuit of anyone. Until you go after knowledge you cannot access knowledge. Knowledge answers to pursuit.

SAVINGS

As the reality of the soon coming famine came to the knowledge of Pharaoh, Joseph and the leaders of Egypt, Egypt began to save food. The first thing Egypt did to checkmate the coming global affliction was to begin saving a major portion of her food production. And so while others were eating up all their food, Egypt was busy saving a major portion of her food.

"Now let Pharaoh look out
for a man discreet and wise
and set him over the land of Egypt.

Let Pharaoh do this,
and let him appoint officers over the land,

*and take the fifth part of the land of
Egypt in the seven plenteous years.*

*And let them gather the food of
those good years that come,
and lay up corn under the hand of Pharaoh,
and let them keep food in the cities.*

*And that food shall be for store to the
land against the seven years of famine,
which shall be in the land of Egypt;
that the land perish not through famine."*

- Genesis 41:33-36

While everyone was busy consuming all they had, Egypt was busy laying up a great portion of all she had in stores against the famine. At the end of the day, it was what Egypt laid up that placed Egypt above the famine and above the scourge of the survival that crippled everyone. While everyone was seriously contending with survival, Egypt was drawing from the abundance of her reserves laid up over time.

GET YOUR OWN STORE

What placed Egypt above the famine and above survival was what she had laid up in store. Those who have nothing laid up, have no business going up. Going up begins with laying up. If you must go up then you must lay up. You don't go up by luck; neither do you go up by chance. You go up by laying up.

If nothing is stored, nothing is sure. Your wealth begins with having your own financial store house. Your store house is your sure house. What Egypt laid up was what kept her. What you keep is what eventually keeps you. What you lay up today is what keeps you tomorrow.

What you save is what eventually saves you. If you have nothing laid up, you will surely come down. The downfall of many today is because many have nothing laid up. It is too dangerous to live without any form of savings. Many practically have nothing stored up.

Laying up today is what prevents coming down tomorrow. In order for you to go up, you must lay up. It will be totally impossible for you to go up in life without laying up. It is totally impossible for you to overcome the scourge of survival without saving. It is impossible for you to defeat poverty without saving.

STAY SAFE

Saving is what puts you above survival. Saving is what takes you beyond survival. Your victory over survival begins with saving. Overcoming survival is impossible without saving. The reason why so many are struggling to survive is because they have no savings. Many are under the grip of survival because they have no savings.

What saved Egypt from the famine was what she had saved. If Egypt had no savings, Egypt would not have been safe. To save is to stay safe. To save is what makes you safe. There is safety in saving. Nothing guarantees your safety in life especially financially like your savings. Your safety is in your savings.

Your safety in life begins with what you save. What you save today is what will save you tomorrow. If you don't have anything saved, you are not safe. Your journey to wealth begins with your savings. If you must have something then you must save something. If you must become something then you must save something.

DON'T EAT EVERYTHING

If you have no savings today, you don't stand a chance tomorrow. Your savings is your back up in life. Your savings is your back up for wealth. The truth about life is that life is fundamentally unpredictable. Anything can happen at anytime to anyone. This is the unfortunate mystery of life. This is why it is best to live your life by faith; believing that everyday will be well.

Just as the day is not complete without the night, in like manner, everyone has his night seasons.

> *"To everything there is a season,
> and a time to every purpose under the heaven:*
>
> *A time to be born, and a time to die;
> a time to plant, and a time to pluck
> up that which is planted;*
>
> *A time to kill, and a time to heal;
> a time to breakdown, and a time to build up."*
>
> – *Eccl. 3:1-3.*

Life is divided into seasons and the reason for this is so that there can always be a balance. Bearing this in mind, wisdom demands that you don't eat up everything you have. You must learn to consume and remain. You must learn to eat and save. If you eat everything, you will end up with nothing.

Those who are wealthy don't eat everything they have. One of the fundamental habits of the wealthy is that they save more than they eat. They save more than they spend. What the wealthy eat or spend is nothing compared to what they save. Regardless of your situation, if you must become wealthy, you must learn to save.

THE DISCIPLINE

Saving is not a choice. Saving is a must. You must learn to eat and remain. This is the fundamental discipline of wealth. The major discipline of wealth is saving. You cannot eat everything you have neither can you consume everything that comes your way.

Eating everything brings anyone to poverty. Spending everything brings anyone to poverty. Consuming everything keeps anyone poor. To eat everything is to stay poor and to spend everything is to remain poor. A portion of all you earn is yours to keep. This is the fundamental law that initiates the release of wealth. This is the core discipline of wealth.

Until you imbibe the discipline of saving, you are not ready for wealth. Saving is a discipline-a compulsory discipline. There is no way around it.

Without this discipline, you will remain poor. Wealth disciplines. One principal thing you will learn as you make your journey towards wealth is discipline. Wealth will teach you discipline.

If you are not disciplined, wealth will be very hard for you to access. This is why wealth is not for just anyone. Wealth is not for everyone. Wealth is for those who are disciplined. It is impossible to access wealth or keep wealth without discipline. The elementary basics of wealth is discipline. You will naturally become disciplined if you desire wealth.

WEALTH IS NOT FOR CHILDREN

When Joseph was counseling Pharaoh on the need to save, Joseph emphatically made it clear that a **MAN** and not a boy or a child should be appointed to handle the entire savings of Egypt.

> *"Now therefore, let Pharaoh look
> out a MAN discreet and wise,
> and set him over the land of Egypt."*
>
> *– Genesis 41:33.*

It was not a boy or a child that was mentioned in respect to savings. It was a man that was mentioned. It takes maturity to save. It takes maturity to eat and remain. It takes maturity not spend every dime you have. It is childish to spend everything you have. Savings is a product of maturity. Your ability to save lies in your maturity.

Your ability to keep a part of what you earn is maturity. Maturity is what makes savings possible. A child cannot save. Savings is not a child's play. Savings is discipline. It is the discipline that leads to wealth. Savings is the discipline that shows maturity.

GROW UP

Savings reveal maturity. It is childishness that makes savings impossible no matter the situation or condition. It is not the lack of money or opportunity but the lack of maturity that makes it impossible to save. It is the lack of maturity that makes anyone unable to save.

Saving is by maturity and not necessarily by opportunity. You don't need an opportunity to save. You need maturity to save. Maturity is what prompts saving. Saving is a sign of maturity. Saving is a proof of maturity. More so, saving is not something you jump into; savings is something you grow into. You begin by saving little and grow from little to great.

Your ability to save is a test on your maturity. Your ability to save is what measures your maturity. This is why for you to come out of survival, you need to grow up. And saving is surely a major part of growing up.

STRATEGIC RELATIONSHIPS

When the famine came, everyone except Egypt was affected. Even Jacob and his entire covenant household were not exempted from the famine. Jacob and his household, like others, had to make several trips to Egypt so that they could survive.

> *"Now when Jacob saw that*
> *there was corn in Egypt,*
> *Jacob said unto his sons,*
> *why do ye look one upon another?*
>
> *And he said, Behold,*
> *I have heard that there is corn in Egypt:*
> *get you down thither, and buy us from thence;*
> *that we may live, and not die.*
>
> *And Joseph's ten brothers went*
> *down to buy corn from Egypt."*
>
> *-Genesis 42:1-3.*

Fortunately for the household of Jacob, it was Joseph their brother who was in charge of food in Egypt. But even when the brothers of Joseph came to buy food from Joseph in Egypt, they could not recognize Joseph their brother. Joseph had changed in so many ways. The little Joseph they knew and sold as a slave to Egypt had really grown up.

More so, even if the brothers of Joseph were told, they would not believe that the same Joseph who out of envy and hatred, they had sold as a slave was now a ruler in Egypt. Joseph now appeared different in the traditional attire of the Egyptians and fluently speaking the language of Egypt. In fact when Joseph was speaking to his brothers, he spoke through an interpreter.

> *"And they said one to another,*
> *we are verily guilty*
> *concerning our brother, in that we saw*
> *the anguish of his soul, when he besought us,*
> *and we would not hear; therefore*
> *is this distress come upon us.*
>
> *And Reuben answered them saying,*
> *spake I not unto you saying,*
> *do not sin against the child;*
> *and ye would not hear? Therefore, behold,*
> *also his blood is required.*
>
> *And they knew not that Joseph*
> *understood them; for he spake unto*
> *them by an interpreter."*
>
> *– Genesis 42:21-23.*

With all these changes, there was no way the brothers of Joseph standing before Joseph, could know that the man before them was their brother. There was nothing to suggest their brotherhood with Joseph. But Joseph recognized them immediately.

> *"And Joseph was the governor over the land,*
> *and he it was that sold to all people of the land;*
> *and Joseph's brethren came and*
> *bowed down themselves before him with*
> *their faces to the earth.*
>
> *And Joseph saw his brethren,*
> *and he knew them, but made himself strange unto them…"*

- Genesis 42:6-7.

So much had changed for Joseph over the years but very little had changed for the brothers of Joseph. For Joseph to have recognized his brothers at an instant, suggests that very little or nothing had changed for his brothers despite their envy and hatred.

The brothers of Joseph, who out of envy and hatred desperately wanted to get rid of their brother Joseph, actually thought that they had succeeded. But time proved them wrong. Time proved and showed how miserable the brothers of Joseph failed in getting rid of Joseph.

ENVY IS BAD

For all those long years when the brothers of Joseph thought that Joseph was gone, nothing really changed for them. There was no tangible change or transformation amongst them. They were very much as they were, with little or no change. That is why hatred is bad. Envy is bad.

Envy hinders progress. Envy hinders change. You can't envy people and be better than people. Envy places you beneath people. Envy makes others to be better than you. Envy robs you of being better. You can't be better with envy. Envy robs you of whatever advantage or initiative you were supposed to have in life.

Eventually, Joseph revealed himself to his brothers and beckoned on them to come with their entire household and stay with him in Egypt.

> *"Then Joseph could not refrain himself*
> *before all them that stood by him;*
> *and he cried, cause every man to go out from me.*
> *And there stood no man with him,*
> *while Joseph made himself known unto his brethren ...*
>
> *And Joseph said unto his brethren,*
> *I am Joseph; doth my father yet live?*
> *And his brethren could not answer him;*
> *for they were troubled at his presence.*

*And Joseph said unto his brethren,
come near to me, I pray you,
and they came near. And he said,
I am your brother Joseph, whom ye sold to Egypt.*

*Now therefore be not grieved,
nor angry with yourselves,
that ye sold me hither:
For God did send me before you to preserve life.*

*For theses two years hath the
famine been in the land:
and yet there are five years,
in the which there shall neither be earing nor harvest.*

*And God sent me before you to
preserve you posterity in the earth,
and to save your lives by a great deliverance.*

*So now it was not you that
sent me hither but God:
and he hath made me a father to pharaoh,
and lord of his household,
and a ruler through out the land of Egypt.*

*Haste ye, and go up to my father,
and say unto him, thus said thy son Joseph,
God hath made me lord of all Egypt:
come down unto me tarry not:*

*And thou shall dwell in the land of Goshen,
and thou shall be near unto me,
thou, and thy children,
and thy children's children, and thy flocks,
and thy herds, and all that thou hast."*

– Genesis 45:1, 3-10.

With Joseph's revelation of himself to his brothers and his eventual invitation to the entire household of Jacob, Jacob and his entire household relocated from Canaan to Egypt. As Jacob and his household stayed with Joseph in Egypt, they were all nourished by Joseph.

> *"And Joseph nourished his father, and his brethren, and all his father's household, with bread, according to their families."*
>
> *– Genesis 47:12.*

No more was Jacob and his household to look for food like the rest. No more was Jacob and his family to struggle to survive any more. They were now nourished daily by Joseph. As people struggled to survive due to the impending famine, Jacob and his entire household were now exempted from struggling to survive all because of Joseph.

Jacob and his household were now living above survival. Survival was no longer a challenge to Jacob and his household as it was before. Jacob and his household had now overcome survival. And the reason they were able to overcome survival was because they were related to Joseph.

DON'T JUST RELATE

Joseph's relationship with Jacob took Jacob and his entire household above survival. Joseph's relationship with Jacob gave Jacob and his household victory over poverty and survival. It was relationship that empowered Jacob and his household to rise above survival.

One of the greatest forces that enables anyone anywhere to overcome survival and by extension poverty is strategic relationship. The kind of relationships you have will either keep you struggling to survive or will take you staying above survival. Nothing connects you to wealth like relationships. Nothing gives you access to wealth like relationships. And nothing keeps you poor like relationships.

BECOME STRATEGIC

Poverty is a product of poor relationships or no relationships and wealth is a product of rich relationships-strategic relationships. Relationship determines wealth. Relationship also determines poverty. A man is poor because his relationships are poor and a man is rich because he has rich relationships.

Poor relationships keep a man perpetually rooted in the cycle of poverty. Poor relationships can keep anyone pinned to the flow of poverty. This is why the people in your life are principally the forces that determine the situations in your life. The people in your life are the ultimate forces that determine your life; whether you will be rich or poor.

The people in your life are basically the ones that determines the direction of your life. Relationship determines situations. Relationship determines destiny. Relationship determines direction. Relationship determines destination. Relationship determines everything. Relationship is powerful.

"He that walketh with wise men shall be wise: but a companion of fools shall be destroyed."

– Proverbs 13:20.

Who you walk with is what determines what you will become. Your friend is what determines your end. Your association is what determines your destination. Your company is what determines your destiny. No man can escape the reality of the people in his life. So many are where they are today because of the kind of people in their lives. Many are struggling today all because of the calibre of relationships they keep.

IT IS NOT BY FORCE

Nothing influences a man like relationships. Nothing determines a man like relationships. Nothing shapes a man like relationships. If you are in a wrong relationship, wrong things will just keep happening to you and if you are in a good relationships, good things will keep happening to you. If the people in your life are wrong then your life will be wrong.

Whether you will fly or fry, it is determined by the relationships you keep. Evil flows through relationships. Good also flows through relationships. Poverty flows through relationships and wealth flows through relationships. This is why you must be very careful of the kind of relationships you keep.

You must be very careful of the kind of people you permit into your life. You must be very selective and not sentimental about your relationships. If you allow sentiments, you will have detriments. Twenty children cannot play together for twenty years. Relationship is not by force. Relationship is by choice. Friendship is not by force but by choice.

Everyone in your life will either add to you or take away from you. They will either multiply you or divide you. Nobody enters your life and leaves you the same. Relationships don't leave you the same. Relationships are meant to be a blessing to you and not a lesson to you.

A BLESSING OR A LESSON

Any relationship that is not a blessing to you will surely become a lesson to you. Any relationship that is not a blessing to you should not be encouraged. Don't bring sentiments into your relationships. Anyone relating with you is affecting and influencing your life. As such, matters like relationships that affects and influences your life should not carry or entertain sentiments.

You must be careful and prayerful as you allow people into your life. Look at the relationship between Joseph and Jacob. Jacob was becoming poor as a result of the famine; Joseph was rich; not just rich but super rich. Jacob and his household were struggling to survive; Joseph was living in super abundance.

Joseph had power, influence and authority over Egypt and the rest of the world; Jacob didn't have such powers. There were clear differences between Jacob and Joseph that went beyond age. Those who are struggling to survive like Jacob cannot help you come out of the rat race called survival and that is because they also need help.

Joseph was able to change the status of Jacob because Joseph was not like Jacob; Joseph was far different from Jacob. Darkness cannot change darkness. A drowning man cannot help another drowning man; if he tries it, they will both drown. Until a man has been helped, he cannot help another. Until a man has been changed, he cannot change another.

BLACK CANNOT CHANGE BLACK

Only those who have been helped can help others. Only those who are different from you can make a difference in you. Anyone who is not different from you cannot make a difference in you. Any one in your shoes cannot change your shoes. It takes a man with a different shoe from yours to change your shoe.

Those in the same level with you cannot help you change your level. Those in the same situation with you cannot help you change your situation. Those struggling to survive cannot help you overcome survival. Only those who have overcome survival can help you overcome survival. This is why you must be very strategic in forging your relationships.

Learn to relate with those who have the testimony you desire. Learn to relate with those whose lives are a picture of the future you seek. Learn to relate with those you admire. Relate with purpose.

SERVICE TO GOD

Another set of people who were exempted from the famine that hit the whole world were the priests. While everyone was struggling to survive, the priests were at rest. The priests had their portion of food given to them daily. The priests were not permitted to suffer.

The priests were not allowed to struggle like the others. The priests only heard of the famine; they only saw the famine but they never felt or experienced the famine. Isn't that amazing?

> *"And Joseph bought all the*
> *land of Egypt for Pharaoh;*
> *for the Egyptians sold every man his field,*
> *because the famine prevailed over them:*
> *so the land became Pharaoh's.*

*And as for the people,
he removed them to cities,
from one end of the borders of Egypt
even to the other end thereof.*

*Only the land of the priests
bought he not: for the priests
had a portion assigned them of Pharaoh,
and did eat their portion which
Pharaoh gave them: wherefore
they sold not their lands."*

– Genesis 47:20-22.

While everybody was busy sweating it out with the struggle to survive, the priests were placed above survival. What affected everyone did not affect the priests. What crippled everyone did not come close to the priests. Not one priest became a victim to the famine.

Who are the priests? The priests are those who are dedicated to the things of God. They are those who are committed to the service of God. One sure force that empowers a man to overcome survival is service to God. Your service to God empowers you to stay above survival.

Listen to this:

*"If they obey and serve him,
they shall spend their days in prosperity
and their years in pleasures."*

– Job 36:11.

Your dedication to the things of God is a sure guarantee to your victory over survival. Your service to God is your sure ticket out of the rat race called survival. You can't truly serve God and still remain a victim of survival. Survival bows to kingdom service. Poverty submits to kingdom service. Prosperity is your guaranteed promise for your service to God.

Service to God will surely deliver prosperity. Your service to God is your journey to a life of prosperity.

In the days of Joshua, when the children of Israel wanted to crossover Jordan to conquer Jericho, the Lord commanded the priests to bear the ark and move in front of the whole nation of Israel.

> *"And then the LORD said unto Joshua,*
> *This day will I begin to magnify*
> *thee in the sight of all Israel,*
> *that may know that, as I was with Moses,*
> *so will I be with thee:*
>
> *And thou shalt command the priests*
> *that bear the ark of the covenant, saying,*
> *When ye are come to the brink of the water of Jordan,*
> *ye shall stand still in Jordan."*
>
> *– Joshua 3:7-8.*

The priests are the ark bearers. They carry the Ark of the Covenant. Before the Lord commanded the priests to bear the ark, they were already bearing the ark. Bearing the ark was not an event for the priests. Bearing the ark was a duty to the priests. Bearing the ark was a lifestyle; a way of life for the priests.

The ark was the business of the priests. Service to God means carrying the ark of God. Service to God means making the things of God your business. Service to God means making the things of God your duty. Service to God, means making the business of God your way of life.

Kingdom service is not a name nor is it an office. No! Kingdom service is a dedication; a commitment to the things of God. One sure thing that positions a man to come out of survival is to make God's work your duty.

DIVINE INTERVENTION

There are clear cases and instances where people must have tried everything and yet overcoming survival still seems impossible. Sometimes, it takes divine intervention to overcome survival. Sometimes, it takes God pulling you out of the rat race of survival by Himself.

Just as there was a famine in the days of Joseph, there was equally also another famine, long after the days of Joseph. This famine was only upon the city of Samaria.

"And there was a great famine in Samaria: and, behold, they besieged it, until an ass's head was sold for fourscore pieces of silver, and the fourth part of a cab of dove's dung for five pieces of silver."

– 11Kings 6:25.

Everyone affected by this famine were all looking for help but no one could help anyone. No human strategy could beat this famine. Every human experience or wisdom failed. Samaria was helpless at the mercy of the famine until God intervened. And when God intervened, the helpless situation of Samaria was turned around.

"Then Elisha said, Hear ye the word of the LORD; Thus saith the LORD, tomorrow about this time shall a measure of fine flour be sold for a shekel, and two measures of barley for a shekel, in the gate of Samaria."

– 11Kings 7:1.

Sometimes, overcoming survival goes beyond human abilities. Sometimes, it goes beyond what you can do. Sometimes, going beyond survival goes beyond human strategies and wisdom. Sometimes, it takes God pulling you out by himself out of the grip of survival. But God does not intervene by luck. God does not intervene by chance.

Certain forces bring the intervention of God to bear in the life of anyone. Bringing God into your situation is not hard at all. All you need is to know how to bring God into your situation.

There was a marriage in Cana of Galilee and Jesus was invited to this marriage.

*"And the third day there
was marriage in Cana of Galilee;
and the mother of Jesus was there:*

*And both Jesus was called, and
his disciples, to the marriage.*

*And when they wanted wine, the mother
of Jesus saith unto him, They have no wine.*

*Jesus said unto her, woman,
what have I to do with thee?
My hour is not yet come?*

*His mother said unto the servants,
whatsoever he said unto you, do it.*

*And there were set there six waterpots
of stone after the purifying of the Jews,
containing two or three firkins apiece.*

*Jesus said unto them,
fill the waterpots with water.
And they filled them up to the brim.*

*And he saith unto them,
draw out now and bear unto the
governor of the feast. And they bare it.*

*When the ruler of the feast had tasted
the water that was made wine, and knew*

*not whence it was: (but the servants which
drew the water knew) the governor of the
feast called the bridegroom,*

*And saith unto him,
Every man at the beginning doth set
forth good wine: and when men have
well drunk, then that which is worse:
but thou hast kept the good wine until now."*

– John 2:1-10.

If Jesus had not intervened when the wine finished, there would have been no more wine and that would have affected the marriage feast. But because of the intervention of Jesus, the wine which had finished was restored back.

Two things brought about the miraculous intervention of Jesus at the marriage feast.

THE PRESENCE OF JESUS

If Jesus was not present at the marriage, Jesus would not have been able to restore the finished wine. It was because Jesus was present at the marriage that was why he was able to intervene. And the reason why Jesus was present was because Jesus was invited to the marriage. Jesus did not just bump into the feast neither did Jesus gate-crash into the feast nor did He just badge into the feast.

Jesus was there because He was invited. If Jesus was not invited, Jesus would never have been there. Jesus will never be in a place he is not invited.

*"And both Jesus was called,
and his disciples, to the marriage."*

– John 2:2

His presence is by your invitation.

A lot of people want God to intervene in their lives and situations but yet they have not invited Him into their lives. The intervention of Jesus was as a result of the presence of Jesus. Divine intervention begins with divine presence. Divine presence is the foundation for divine intervention.

Divine presence is what triggers divine intervention. For God to intervene, God must be present. Until God is present, God cannot do anything for you. It is not your situation that moves God to work; it is his presence that moves Him to work on your behalf.

GOD CAN INTERVENE

It is the presence of God in you that opens you up to the interventions of God. And so God has to step into your life if God must intervene in your life. Nothing just happens. Everything that happens is made to happen. Divine intervention is not by luck or accident. Divine intervention is by divine presence.

Until God is present, God cannot intervene. Only His presence can guarantee His intervention. And His presence is by your personal and sincere invitation. Just as divine intervention is by divine presence, divine presence is by personal invitation. Until you invite God into your life, God will not come into your life. And until God comes into your life, God cannot intervene on your behalf.

By and large, divine intervention begins with a personal invitation from you to God. For God to intervene in your life, God must be invited into your life. For God to do something in your life, God must be invited into your life. Everything boils down to your inviting God into your life. Your personal invitation to God is the foundation for God's intervention in your life.

THE ISSUE OF THE WINE

Your personal invitation to God is what positions you for God's intervention. God's intervention is based on your personal invitation. Without your personal invitation to God, divine intervention is clearly impossible. You must reach out to God if God is to reach out to you. Stop waiting for God. God is waiting for you.

It would have been an assumption that because Jesus was at the marriage, He would just intervene without Mary bringing the issue of the finished wine to Him. That assumption would have been a very big mistake. That assumption would have been grossly misleading.

Despite the fact that Jesus was at the marriage, when the wine finished, Mary did not just assume that Jesus would intervene. Instead, Mary took advantage of the presence of Jesus at the marriage and approached Jesus with the issue of the finished wine. A lot of people have God in their lives and they just assume that because God is in their lives He will just intervene in their lives and situation.

ASSUMPTION IS A KILLER

Instead of personally taking their problems to God, they assume that God will just intervene; and so they get disappointed when God does not intervene. Instead of people taking advantage of the presence of God in their lives by bringing their situations to God, they place assumptions on the presence of God in their lives.

It is not enough for God to be in your life. Like Mary, if you want God to intervene in your situation, then you must take your situation to Him. Beyond inviting God into your life, you must invite God into your situation. Inviting God into your life is the first step.

Inviting God into your situation is the next step-another step towards your testimony. Until God is invited into a situation, God cannot change that situation. Stop placing assumptions on God. Start taking advantage of God. God is in your life for your advantage and not for your assumption.

To assume God is very dangerous. As long as you continue to assume that God will do something, God will do nothing. God does not work by your assumptions. God works by your invitations.

Listen to this story:

*"And the same day, when the even
was come, he saith unto them,
Let us pass over to the other side.*

*And when they hath sent away the
multitude, they took him even as he
was in a ship. And there were also
with him other little ships.*

*And there arose a great storm of wind,
and the waves beat into the ship,
so that it was now full.*

*And he was in the hinder part of the ship,
asleep on a pillow: and they awake him, and say
unto him, Master, carest thou not that we perish?*

*And he arose, and rebuked the wind,
and said unto the sea, Peace be still. And the wind
ceased, and there was a great calm."*

– Mark 4:35-39.

As the storm beat against the ship of the disciples, the disciples just assumed that with Jesus on board, the storm will just cease. But Jesus went to sleep. Jesus was inactive. The disciples just imagined that Jesus cannot be on board with the storm beating against the ship. But as they continued to assume, Jesus continued to sleep.

PRAY ABOUT EVERYTHING

Sleeping refers to a state of inactivity. Jesus was inactive. Nothing makes God inactive in the life of anyone like assumptions. Assumption makes God inactive. Assumption makes God appear to be sleeping. A lot of people have Jesus in their lives but Jesus is sleeping in their situation.

They imagine that with Jesus in their lives, these storms ought not to be. The disciples of Jesus continued in their assumptions until they woke Jesus up. It was when they brought Jesus to the scene that Jesus prevailed over the storm. The time has come for you to wake Jesus up in your life.

The time has come for you to put Jesus to action in your life. Don't just assume that God knows about your situation. Make sure God knows about your situation by personally taking your situation to God in prayers. And as you take your situation to God in prayers, you open up yourself for divine intervention.

JOURNEY TO WEALTH

WEALTH IS FUNDAMENTALLY A PERSONAL CHOICE

BY: JOSHUA GREAT

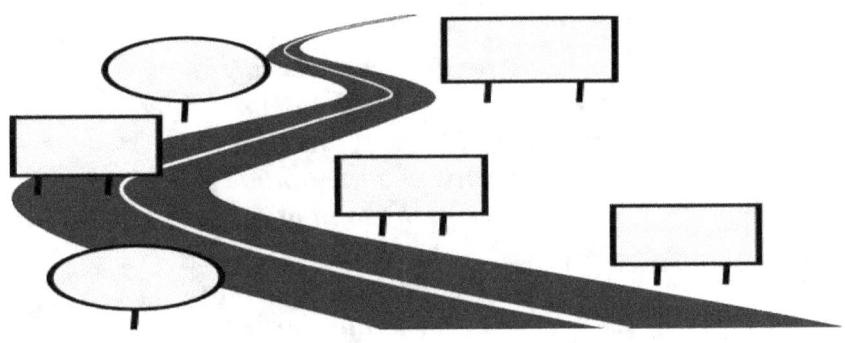

CHAPTER TWO
THE CORE

As the famine continued, the world trooped down to Egypt for survival. And as people trooped down to Egypt; they were not going down to Egypt to get food for free. The food in Egypt was for sale.

> *"And famine was over all the face of the earth: and Joseph opened all the storehouses, and sold unto the Egyptians, and the famine waxed sore in the land of Egypt.*
>
> *And all countries came into Egypt to Joseph for to buy corn; because that the famine was so sore in all lands."*
>
> *– Genesis 41:56-57.*

Everyone came to buy from Egypt. Every country, every tribe, every race; they all came to buy food from Egypt. With the money of everyone in the land of Egypt, Egypt emerged as the wealthiest nation on earth. Egypt became the richest country in the world. The wealth of Egypt swelled and multiplied with every passing day.

Without any disputation Egypt emerged as the world's number one financial power house. Egypt's wealth was not a thing of luck. Egypt's wealth was not a gamble or a game. Egypt's wealth was as result of certain key forces.

WEALTH IS A CONTRIBUTION

While everyone was spending, Egypt was gathering. While everyone was releasing their finances to Egypt, Egypt was increasing by the release of the finance of everyone. The famine brought a platform for everyone to contribute to the wealth of Egypt.

Egypt grew wealthy with the dogged contributions of everybody. Wealth is simply the contributions of many into the lives of a few. Wealth is having the contributions of many. Wealth is securing the contributions of many. Wealth is earning the contributions of many.

Your wealth lies in making people contribute into your life. Your wealth lies in making people give to you. If you can make people give to you, you will surely emerge wealthy. If you can secure the contributions of people, you will become wealthy.

PEOPLE MUST GIVE TO YOU

The wisdom of harnessing the contributions of people into your life is what births wealth into your life. Your ability to make people release their substance to you is what makes you emerge wealthy. Everyone who is wealth anywhere, is that person who has earned the profound ability of making people contribute into their lives.

If you must stay above poverty, you must know how to make people contribute to you. The giving of people into the life of a person is what makes wealth possible in the life of that person. You must know how to make people give to you; not by begging; not by lobbying; not by gimmicks; not by manipulation; not by dirty pranks or deception but by mastering the ancient secrets of attracting and commanding from many. It is an attraction and its possible.

Look at Job.

Job was described in scriptures as the wealthiest man in his time and days. No one was as rich as Job. No one could stand the wealth of Job. Job's wealth towered above everyone's wealth. Job had no equal.

> *"There was a man in the land of Uz,*
> *whose name was Job. And that man*
> *was perfect and upright and one that*
> *feared God, and eschewed evil.*
>
> *And there were born unto him*
> *seven sons and three daughters*

> *His substance also was seven
> thousand sheep, and three thousand camels,
> and five hundred yoke of oxen, five hundred
> she asses, and a very great household; so that
> this man was the greatest of all the men of the east."*
>
> *– Job 1:1-3.*

This was the wealth of Job. Substance upon substance, without equal to anyone, made Job the wealthiest of all men. But somewhere along the line, all of Job's great wealth vanished. Every investment and substance Job ever had, got caught up with the wind of destruction. Disaster upon disaster visited Job until Job lost everything he had including his family.

> *"And there came a messenger unto Job,
> and said, The oxen were plowing, and
> the asses feeding besides them:*
>
> *And the Sabeans fell upon them,
> and took them away: yea they have
> slain the servants with the edge of the swords:
> and I only am escaped alone to tell thee.*
>
> *While he was yet speaking, there
> came also another, and said,
> The fire of God, is fallen from heaven,
> and hath burned up the sheep, and the
> servants, and consumed them; and I only
> am escaped alone to tell thee.*
>
> *While he was yet speaking,
> there came also another, and said,
> The Chaldeans made out three bands,
> and fell upon the camels, and have
> carried then away, yea, and slain
> the servants with the edge of the sword,*

and I only am escaped to tell thee.

*While he was yet speaking,
there came also another, and said,
Thy sons and thy daughters were eating
and drinking wine in their eldest brother's house.*

*And, behold, there came a great wind
from the wilderness, and smote the four
corners of the house, and it fell upon
the young men, and they are dead; and I only am
escaped alone to tell thee.*

*Then Job arose, and rent his mantle,
and shaved his head, and fell down upon the
ground, and worshipped."*

– Job 1:14-20.

All manner of calamities brought Job down from the great heights of wealth to the very degrading depths of poverty. Job's wealth was now a thing of the past. Job, who used to be the richest, was now the poorest.

Job's situation was so pathetic. Everyone deserted Job. Friends, colleagues, acquaintances and even relations-they all left Job. Even Job's wife grew tired of Job's situation so much so that she busted out and mocked Job's loyalty to God.

*"Then said his wife unto him;
Dost thou still retain thine integrity?
curse God, and die.*

*But he said unto her, Thou speakest
as one of the foolish women speaketh.
What? Shall we receive good at the hand of God,
and shall we not receive evil? In all this
did not Job sin with his lips."*

-Job 2:9-10.

Prosperity attracts friends but adversity tries them. Nothing tries people like adversity. Adversity tries people and reveals them for who they really are. This is why adversity brings revelations. Nothing can be hidden from fire. Fire exposes and disposes.

Everyone disassociated from Job. Job was now alone; treated like a leper. Such was the cruel condition of Job. Even when Job's friends came to visit Job after hearing of the evils that visited him, they could not recognize Job. The calamities that befell Job had terribly disfigured Job.

> *"Now when Job's three friends heard of all this evils that was come upon him, they came everyone from his own place; Eliphaz the Temanite, and Bildad the Shuhite, and Zophar the Naamathite: for they had made an appointment together to come to mourn with him and to comfort him.*
>
> *And when they lifted up their eyes afar off, and knew him not, they lifted up their voice, and wept: and they rent everyone his mantle, and sprinkled dust upon their heads towards heaven.*
>
> *So they sat down with upon the ground seven days and seven nights, and none spake a word unto him: for they saw that his grief was very great."*

– Job 2:11-13.

Job was now no more recognizable. It was that bad. But despite all the things that happened to Job, Job remained hopeful. Job remained optimistic.

Look at how Job saw himself:

"For there is hope of a tree, if it be cut down,
that it sprout again, and that the tender
branch thereof will not cease.

Though the root thereof wax old in the earth,
and the stock thereof die in the ground;

Yet through the scent of water it will bud,
and bring forth boughs like a plant."

-Job 14:7-9.

What a way to be hopeful. Job knew that no condition or situation is forever. Somehow, change will surely come one day. And change did come for Job. Job rose again. Job bounced back to life again. Job became rich again and was even richer than he was before.

"And the LORD turned the captivity of Job . . .
also the LORD gave Job twice as much as he had before."

– Job 42:10.

But how did Job become wealthy again so much so that he had twice as much as what he had before? How did Job bounce back from adverse poverty to immense wealth? He was the richest, then became the poorest and then became the richest again. Not too many people can do that.

Not too many people can actually bounce back. Only very few can actually bounce back after such a great calamity. Only very few can actually return from hell and live to tell the experience. Hell is not only in eternity. Hell is also an experience. What Job went through was pure hell.

Just like Job, so many go through hell but get stucked in hell. They want to come out but they can't. Coming out of hell is not an easy task. So many don't get to come out. This is why bouncing back is not an easy task. And so, how did Job do it? How did Job bounce back?

What was the secret to Job's wealth again? What was the key element to Job's wealth again? Job's restoration back to wealth was certainly not by luck. Something triggered Job's restoration back to wealth.

This is it -

"Then came there unto him all his brethren, all his sisters, and all they that had been of his acquaintance before, and did eat bread with him in his house: and they bemoaned him, and comforted him over all the evil that the LORD hath brought upon him: every man also gave him a piece of money, and everyone an earring of gold."

– Job 42:11.

Job's restored wealth was a product of people giving into the life of Job. When God wanted to change Job's situation, God caused everyone to give into the life of Job. Job became rich again by the various contributions of people into his life. Everybody gave Job money.

Everyone gave Job something. If everyone in your city or state gives you money, how wealthy will you be? Once again wealth is in the ability to harness the various resources of people into your life. Wealth is in the ability to draw from people. Wealth is in the ability to tap from people.

People contributing to someone is what makes anyone wealthy. Everyone who is wealthy is principally a recipient of men. Everyone who is wealthy, is an embodiment of the various contributions of people.

YOU NEED PEOPLE

It is people that makes anyone wealthy. Everyone who is wealthy anywhere, is primarily a product of people. This is why it is totally impossible to become wealthy without people. Wealth is impossible without people. The first key element to wealth is people.

The fundamental secret to wealth is people. If you can get people you can get wealth. If you can connect with people, you will connect with wealth. Without people, there is no wealth. This is the secret to wealth and this secret is as ancient as life itself. Only those who understand this secret will have easy access to wealth.

People are the secrets to wealth. If you can access people, you can access wealth. People are your access to wealth. Wealth comes through people. You need people to become wealthy. Without people, wealth is impossible. You need people to command wealth. You need people to possess wealth.

Wealth begins with people and ends with people. Outside people there can be no wealth. Outside people, wealth is only a dream. Outside people, wealth is a big mirage. Wealth lies with people. Wealth flows through people. Wealth is a product of people.

ITS ALL ABOUT ASSOCIATING

This is why wealth does not come by isolation. Wealth comes by association. Association is the principal force behind wealth. Association is the backbone of wealth. People are your keys to wealth. Your access to people is your access to wealth. People are your ladder to wealth.

If you know your way with people, you will never have a problem with wealth. Wealth is cheap with people. Wealth is easy with people. Wealth is only possible with people. There is no one who is wealthy anywhere who did not become wealthy through the deliberate efforts of people.

This is why the difference between the wealthy and the poor is people. The difference between becoming wealthy and staying poor is people. **The wealthy have their ways with people while the poor dwell in isolation. The advantage the wealthy have over the poor is association and the major challenge of the poor is isolation.**

Isolation creates poverty. Isolation breeds poverty. Isolation encourages poverty. Poverty flows through isolation. Isolation is the stronghold of poverty. Isolation is the backbone of poverty.

> *"Wealth maketh many friends;*
> *but the poor is separated from his neighbour."*
>
> *– Proverbs 19:4.*

The major problem of the poor is isolation. The major challenge of the poor is isolation. A man is poor not because he lacks money neither is a man poor because he lacks possessions. Rather a man is poor because he lacks people. The one who has no one is actually no one.

Wealth comes from people. The lack of money or possessions does not truly define poverty nor does it really determine poverty. True poverty is in the lack of people and not in the lack of money. The lack of people is the real definition of poverty. Anyone who has no one is no one. Anyone who has no one is the one who is truly poor. Such a person is to be pitied. Such a person, is of all men, most miserable.

Wealth is not just in having money. Wealth is not just in having properties and possessions. That is the supposed surface reality of wealth. Wealth goes beyond having money. Wealth goes beyond having possessions. Wealth is deeper than having material things.

True wealth is in having people. The wealth of a man lies in the people in his life. People define wealth. People determine wealth. Your wealth is people. It does not matter what you have, if you don't have people, you don't have anything. If you don't have anyone, you don't have anything but if you have someone, you have something. Wealth is in people and not in money or buildings.

ISOLATION IS A PLAGUE

You need someone to become someone. Whatever you have or think you have, is totally irrelevant without people. Whatever you have is useless without people. Nothing in this life is ever useful without people. Nothing in this life is truly relevant without people. Nothing in this life is of any real significance without people.

Without people, everything is nothing and with people nothing is everything. People are the real substance of wealth. People are the real definitions of wealth. A man's wealth is truly defined by the people in his life. A man's wealth is truly defined by his contacts and connections. When you have people, you have wealth. With people comes wealth.

The challenge of the poor is that they are separated from people and thereby separated from wealth. The dilemma of the poor is that they are disconnected from people and by extension disconnected from the treasures and the resources of people. As such, in dealing with poverty, you must first of all deal with isolation.

NETWORK IS CRUCIAL

For anyone to truly become wealthy, that person needs people. For anyone to access wealth, that person needs to access people. You must first of all acknowledge the fact that you need people to get wealth before you can begin to get wealth.

One major step towards wealth is breaking isolation and embracing association. Wealth begins with associating with people. Wealth begins with networking with people. Wealth is principally a network; a network with people. Wealth is connecting with people. Your connection with people is your connection with wealth.

Your ability to stay connected with people is what gives you access to wealth. Your chance with people is your chance with wealth. When you connect with people, you connect with their resources. When you access people, you access their resources.

THINK OF PEOPLE AND NOT MONEY

Stop thinking of how to get money; start thinking of how to get people. This is the deciding factor. You don't get money by thinking about money. Money does not work or come that way. Rather you get money by thinking about people. Think of how to help people. Think of how to get people. Think of how to connect with people. Think of how to access people.

If you start thinking of people instead of money, you will get money faster than you hope or expect. The poor thinks of how to get money while the rich thinks of how get people. You cannot get money until you get people. The way to money is through people. Getting people is getting money. Getting people is getting wealth. Money cannot exist alone. Money is irrelevant without people. Money has no value without people.

It is people that makes money relevant. It is people that gives value to money. This is why money was made for man and not man for money. The way to money is through people. Your access to money is through people. The money you are looking for is with people. And until you get people you can't get money. The big question is, how do you get people?

THE SECRET OF CONNECTING WITH PEOPLE
How do you connect with people in such a way that you connect with their resources? How do you access people and by extension access their substance and resources, bearing in mind that those who must access wealth must first of all access people?

During the famine years, everybody trooped down to Egypt for food. As everyone trooped down to Egypt for food, they gave their money, treasures and substances to Egypt in exchange for food. And by accessing the resources and treasures of everyone, Egypt emerged as the wealthiest nation in the world.

Egypt associated with everyone. Egypt accessed everyone. Egypt connected with everyone. And the reason why Egypt was able to connect with everyone and by extension connect with their resources was because Egypt had something to offer. Egypt was able to access people because Egypt had something to offer.

What Egypt had to offer was food. In the whole world, Egypt was the only country that had food. As people came for Egypt's food, Egypt had unhindered access to people of all sorts from all over the world.

OFFER SOMETHING

Nothing gives you access to people like what you have to offer to people. Nothing connects you to people like what you have to offer people. What you have to offer is what brings you to people and brings people to you. No one will be interested in someone who has nothing to offer.

No one will want to have any business with anyone who has nothing to offer. As such, isolation which is a core element of poverty is in having nothing to offer. For you to break isolation, you must have something to offer. For you to come out of poverty, you must have something to offer. For you to connect with people, you must have something to offer.

ITS ALL GAIN

The world is not interested in your stories. The world is only interested in what you have to offer. If you have nothing to offer then you cannot prosper. If you have nothing to offer, you will continue to suffer. Your offering is what terminates your suffering. If you have nothing to offer, no one will be really interested in you.

For every relationship, there must be something to take and something at stake. For every relationship, there must be something to gain. If there is nothing to gain; if there is nothing at stake, then there will be no relationship; there will be no interest. Interest comes with gain. That is how the human psychology works.

If people or someone must be interested in you, then there must something to gain. Gain is the bait of interest. Gain is what secures interest. Where there is no gain, there will be no interest. Therefore, all relationships must have something to gain and something at stake for this is the beginning of every great and meaningful enterprise.

WEALTH BEGINS WITH THIS

Wealth begins with having something to offer. To have nothing to offer is to have nothing. What makes anyone wealthy anywhere is in having something to offer. And what makes anyone poor anywhere is in having nothing to offer.

The poor have nothing to offer. Anyone who has nothing to offer will have nothing but poverty. Your wealth is in what you have to offer. What you have to offer is what determines how wealthy you will be. You don't become wealthy by luck.

You don't become wealthy by chance. It is what you have to offer that determines your wealth. The difference between the wealthy and the poor is in what the wealthy has to offer that the poor does not have. The wealthy always has something to offer.

If you must become wealthy, you must have something to offer to people. You cannot become wealthy without having something to offer. What can you offer? What do you have to offer? If you can offer something then you can become something.

THERE IS SOMETHING TO OFFER

It is what you have to offer that positions you for wealth. Those who are wealthy anywhere, are wealthy because they are offering something to people. When you offer something to people, people will offer treasures to you. Wealth begins with having something to offer.

You must have something to offer. It could be a service, a product, a skill, a talent, an experience, an idea, an insight, a discovery; you must have something to offer. Your access to wealth lies in what you have to offer.

Look at Lazarus.

Lazarus is undoubtedly one of the poorest men in the whole of the scriptures. Lazarus is a clear definition of poverty. Lazarus is a clear characterization of poverty. Every detail and description of Lazarus is nothing but poverty.

*"There was a certain rich man,
which was clothed in purple and fine linen,
and fared sumptuously everyday:*

*And there was a certain beggar
named Lazarus, which was laid*

at the gate, full of sores.

And desiring to be fed with the crumbs which fell from the rich man's table: moreover the dogs came and licked his sores."

– Luke 16:19-21.

This was the pathetic story of Lazarus. Lazarus had nothing to offer and so Lazarus suffered. Those who have nothing to offer will continue to suffer. It is what you have to offer that stops your suffering. Your offering is what stops your suffering. Your offering is what terminates your suffering.

So many are suffering and languishing in poverty all because they have nothing to offer. Having nothing to offer is choosing to suffer. If you offer nothing, you will suffer something. Lazarus' only desire was to beg from the rich man. Lazarus had nothing to offer and so no one connected or identified with Lazarus.

Day in day out, Lazarus sat at the gate of the rich man to beg for crumbs from the rich man's table. Lazarus' only desire was to beg for leftovers. Lazarus was not handicapped or deformed in anyway but Lazarus chose to beg. Lazarus' only dream was to beg. His focus everyday were the leftovers from the rich man's table.

STOP DEPENDING ON PEOPLE

Without the rich man, Lazarus will not have anything to eat. Without the rich man, Lazarus will not feed. The rich man was Lazarus' only hope. And so Lazarus depended on the rich man for food. Lazarus depended on the rich man for survival. As Lazarus continued to depend on the rich man for food, Lazarus continued to remain poor.

Lazarus' dependence on the rich did not change Lazarus' situation rather it worsened his situation. One key thing about Lazarus was that he was totally dependent on the rich man for survival. And it was Lazarus' total dependence on the rich man that kept Lazarus poor.

If only Lazarus could stop depending on the rich man and rather focus on offering something to the rich man, or to the people around him, Lazarus's would have had a far better life. One major character of poverty is that poverty makes a man depend on people especially for survival.

Anything that makes you depend on any one for anything will surely make you poor. Depending on people for food; depending on people for money; are all forms and shades of poverty. Until you break your dependence on people, you have not broken your link with poverty.

LEARN TO BECOME SOMEONE

Until you stop depending on people for food; for money; for survival, you have not started your journey to wealth. Until you stop depending on people, you cannot become wealthy. Wealth begins with independence. Anything that makes you depend on anybody for anything will surely rob you of the privilege of becoming somebody.

Anything that makes you depend on anyone for anything will surely stop you from becoming someone in life. Depending on anyone will surely deprive you of becoming someone. Becoming someone begins with depending on no one. This may sound hash and hard but it is the way it is. You are not serious to become someone in life as long as you are still depending someone.

You are not ready for a life of your own as long as you are still depending on someone. Until you stop depending on someone or anyone, you are not ready for whatever good life has to offer. Anything that makes you depend on anybody for anything only places you at the mercy of that person which in turn makes you vulnerable.

Wealth does not place you at the mercy of others rather wealth places others at your mercy. Just as Lazarus was at the mercy of the rich man, wealth does not make you vulnerable. Wealth gives you strength.

> *"The rich man's wealth is his strong city:*
> *the destruction of the poor is their poverty."*

– Proverbs 10:15.

It is totally impossible for you to depend on people and still access wealth. Your access to wealth begins with breaking your dependence on people. You must have a mind of your own. You must have a voice of your own. You must have a stand of your own.

You must have a will of your own. You must have a plan of your own. You must have a dream of your own. You must have a life of your own. You must have your own. Stop living for people; start living your own life. Stop living the dreams of others; start living your own dreams.

Refuse to remain a shadow. Refuse to remain in the shadows of people. You are not a shadow. Whatever must become real must not remain a shadow. Whatever must be felt must not remain a shadow. Whatever must be certain must not remain a shadow.

Shadows are not real. Shadows are shades with no form or reality or certainty. There is no reality with shadows. There is no certainty with shadows.

LEAVE THE SHADOWS OF OTHERS

Those who depend on people most times get deceived by people. Those who depend on people most times get used and betrayed by people. Those who depend on people don't always rise above people. Your rise above people begins with breaking your dependence on people. Your rise in life begins with your independence in life.

For a very long time, Jacob depended on Laban for food, for survival, for money; for everything. Even as a married man with children, Jacob still depended on Laban. At a certain period, Laban would give Jacob a token called wages. This arrangement continued for a long time until one day, Jacob, burdened with the task of meeting the ever growing needs of his large family, decided to stop depending on Laban. He decided to put his own life in his hands.

"And it came to pass when Rachel had born Joseph, that Jacob said unto Laban, send me away, that I may go unto

my own place, and to my country.

*Give me my wives an my children for
whom I have served thee, and let me go:
for thou knowest my service which I have done thee.*

*And Laban said unto him, I pray thee,
if I have found favor in thine eyes,
tarry: for I have learned by experience
that the LORD hath blessed me for thy sake.*

And he said, Appoint me thy wages, and I will give it.

*And he said unto him,
Thou knowest how I have served thee,
and how thy cattle was with me.*

*For it was little which thou hast
before came, and it is now increased
into a multitude: and the LORD hath
blessed thee since my coming: and now
when shall I provide for my own house also?"*

– Genesis 30:25-30.

It would have taken so much guts for Jacob to declare to Laban that he was leaving. At the time when Jacob approached Laban that he was leaving with his family, Jacob was seriously struggling to provide for his family. But Jacob knew that depending on Laban was not going to change but worsen his income and situation.

If his income and situation were going to change, then his first step would be to stop depending on Laban and take his life into his own hands. This will take a lot of courage.

THERE IS A RISK AHEAD

It took great courage for Jacob to approach Laban that he was leaving with his large family. It took great courage not because Jacob was afraid of

Laban or was Laban a terror but because the unknown awaited Jacob. When Jacob wanted to leave Laban, the only things Jacob demanded for as recorded by scriptures were his wives and children.

There was no mention of the fact that Jacob demanded for any possession which goes to show that Jacob had no real or tangible possessions. If Jacob was to leave Laban with his very large family, he would have left with no real or tangible possession. That means Jacob had little or nothing as he decided to leave Jacob.

Wherever Jacob was going to, he definitely would have had virtually nothing to start anything with. And with nothing to start anything with, how was Jacob going to cope let alone meet the ever-growing needs of his very large family? That must really be frightening. Even if Jacob had an idea, how was he going to start with practically nothing?

WEALTH IS A RISK

The unknown awaited Jacob as he proposed to leave Laban. But Jacob was not afraid of the unknown. Jacob was ready to tackle the unknown. Jacob embraced the unknown. With the unknown awaiting Jacob and with no real or tangible possessions attached to Jacob, Jacob still approached Laban that he was leaving. This was courage at work.

It is very easy to depend on people but it is very hard to stay without depending on people. Its very difficult to stay independent. With independence, comes the unknown. The unknown always follows independence. And because so many fear the unknown, so many prefer to stay dependent.

THE TASK OF INDEPENDENCE

Better to stay with what you know than to risk what you don't know. This is the prevailing mindset of so many-many who stay dependent on people. The unknown has made so many to remain dependent and hooked on people. This is why independence is hard.

Independence is tough. Independence is not easy at all in anyway. It takes courage-a lot of courage to stop depending on people. Most times, if not all times, poverty is simply a result of the lack of courage. A lot of people lack the courage to stop depending on people.

A lot people lack the courage to face the future. A lot of people lack the courage to take certain risks. A lot of people lack the courage to become wealthy. A lot of people lack the courage to take the necessary steps to move their lives forward.

A lot of people lack the courage to move on. A lot of people lack the courage to take the bull by the horn. A lot of people lack the courage to put their lives in their own hands. Many prefer putting their lives in the hands people.

FACE THE UNKNOWN

Uneasy lies the head that wears the crown. Where courage is lacking, excuses will abound. The many excuses in the lives of so many is as a result of the fact that courage is lacking. A lot of people lack the courage to take their lives into their hands. And the reason why so many lack courage is because so many people don't want to face the unknown.

So many can't handle the unknown. The unknown scares a lot of people. The unknown frightens people. The unknown is severely dreaded by so many. The unknown is a mystery. Fear has kept so many rooted in poverty. Fear has kept so many struggling for survival. Fear (the fear of the unknown) has denied so many the access to wealth. So many people are afraid of the unknown. So many people dread the unknown.

THE FAINT HEARTED HAVE NO PLACE

The fear of the unknown is the bane of poverty. The fear of the unknown has kept a lot of people tied to the grip of poverty. The fear of the unknown has made so many people to settle with poverty instead of venturing into wealth. The fear of the unknown has kept so many people in bondage.

If you fear the unknown, you will remain unknown. Until you embrace the unknown, you will remain unknown. Until you embrace the unknown, you will never be known. Those who are known today, are known because they ventured into the unknown. They embraced the unknown. They were not totally sure that all will work out but they ventured all the same. The unknown is the key to the known. The unknown is the secret to the known.

Wealth is an adventure-an adventure of faith. Wealth is a courage venture. Wealth takes a lot of guts. Wealth takes a lot of courage. Wealth takes a lot. Wealth is not for the faint-hearted. Wealth is not for the chicken-hearted. Wealth is for the lion-hearted. You need courage to access wealth.

IT IS NOT ABOUT BEING PRECISE

Most times, wealth is a venture into the unknown. Wealth is not a calculated destination. Wealth is not mathematics where decisions are based on precisions and calculations. In the journey to wealth, so many calculations go wrong. So many plans fail. So many projections fail. Wealth is not a precision. Wealth is a decision.

Wealth is not a calculation. Wealth is an adventure. Wealth goes beyond calculation. There are many instances where the best of calculations have failed in the pursuit of wealth and success. Wealth is not something you can calculate. Wealth is beyond calculating. Wealth is an undertaking of faith. Wealth goes beyond putting one and one together.

There are so many unknown and undetermined variables in your journey to wealth. So many things will remain unsure and unknown as you make your journey to wealth. It is the unsure and the unknown that scares people and stops people from accessing wealth. But be it as it may, you must not allow the unknown to stop or scare you.

In your journey to wealth, you cannot be sure of everything and you cannot know everything. But despite all these, you must be ready to take your chances. You must be ready to face the unknown. You must be ready to tackle the unknown.

YOU MUST BE READY TO VENTURE

Your journey to wealth will definitely bring you with so many unknown outcomes. The demand of wealth is that, it pushes you into ventures and most of them are principally unknown, uncertain, unsure and unpredictable. If you are not ready to venture, you are not ready for a future. Your future is in your ventures.

If you are not ready to venture, you are not ready for wealth. If you are not ready to venture, you are not ready to prosper. Prospering is in venturing. You must venture if you must prosper. You must venture if you must conquer. If you are not ready for the unknown, you are not ready for wealth. This is where faith comes in. This is where sharp instinct as against precision comes in.

You must learn to have faith. Those who must venture must have faith. Wealth is not just about what is known. Principally, wealth is mostly about what is unknown. Most times, wealth takes you to unknown waters; unknown dimensions. Always remember that those who fear the unknown never become known.

When God told Abraham to leave his father's house and country, God did not tell Abraham where he was going to.

God only said,

"Depart from your father's house to a land I will show you". "A land that I will show you", is not a defined place nor is it a known destination. *"A land that I will show you",* was clearly an unknown place.

> *"Now the LORD said unto Abram,*
> *Get thee out of thy country, and from*
> *thy kindred, and from thy father's house,*
> *unto a land that I will shew thee."*
>
> *– Genesis 12:1.*

Abraham had a very great destiny. All the families of the earth were to be blessed in Abraham.

> *"And I will make of thee a great nation,*
> *and I will bless thee, and make thy name great;*
> *and thou shall be a blessing:*
>
> *And I will bless them that bless thee;*

and curse him that curseth thee:
and in thee shall all families of the earth be blessed."

– Genesis 12:2-3.

This was the greatness awaiting Abraham. But Abraham's journey to greatness was to begin with a venture into the unknown. Abraham's destiny was to begin with a journey into the unknown. Abraham faced the unknown and today Abraham is a reference point all over the world.

Most of life remains unknown. A vast portion of life is still very unknown. With all the innovations, technologies and discoveries, a huge chunk of life still remains unknown. All the innovations and technologies of our world has only given us a minute revelation of life.

So much lies in the deep. So much lies in the unknown. A gigantic part of life's depths is still covered. This is why life will continually remain a mystery. And only ventures can unlock mysteries.

THERE ARE ODDS TO FACE

If Abraham had not ventured, Abraham would not have had a future. There is no future without a venture. If you must have a future, then you must be ready to venture. If you are afraid of the unknown you will remain poor. If you are afraid of the unknown, you will remain wretched. Your access to wealth lies in your venture into the unknown.

You must be ready to venture. You must not be afraid to fail. You must not be afraid to make mistakes. You must not be afraid to lose. You must not entertain these fears because they are all part of the journey. You must be courageous and face the unknown.

The journey to wealth is full of risks, discomfort and many unknown outcomes. If you are not ready for these things then you are not ready for wealth. Don't be comfortable with only what you know. You must learn to face what you don't know. It is not everything that can be predicted or calculated. Wealth is a journey of faith. Wealth is a venture of faith. Wealth is faith and courage at work.

JOURNEY TO WEALTH

WEALTH IS FUNDAMENTALLY A PERSONAL CHOICE

BY: JOSHUA GREAT

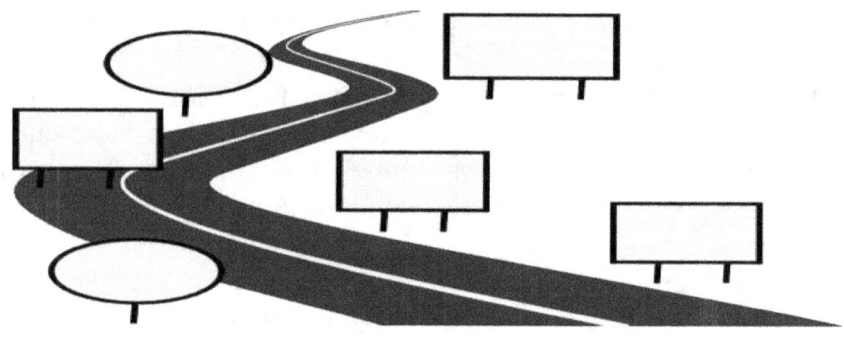

CHAPTER THREE
YOU HAVE IT

When Jacob wanted to leave Laban, Laban refused and told Jacob to name his price. But instead of Jacob accepting Laban's price and still stay dependent on Laban, Jacob came up with an offer for Laban.

"And he said, what shall I give thee?
And Jacob said, thou shall not give
me anything: if thou will do this thing
for me, I will again feed and keep thy flock.

I will pass through all thy flock today,
removing from thence all the speckled and
spotted cattle, and all the brown
cattle among the sheep, and the spotted and
speckled goats amongst the goats: and of such be my hire.

So shall my righteousness answer
for me in time to come, when it shall
come for my hire before thy face,
everyone that is not speckled and
spotted among the goats, and brown
among the sheep, that shall be counted stolen with me.

And Laban, said, Behold, I would it
might be according to thy word.

And he removed that day the he goats,
that were ringstraked and spotted,
and all the she goats that were speckled
and spotted, and everyone that
had some white on it, and all the
brown among the sheep, and gave
them into the hand of his sons.

*And he set three days journey
betwixt himself and Jacob: and Jacob
fed the rest of Laban's flock."*

– *Genesis 30:31-36.*

Laban accepted Jacob's offer. And by Jacob's offer to Laban, Jacob became so rich and had so much possessions.

*"And the man increased exceedingly,
and had much cattle, and maidservants,
and menservants, and camels and asses."*

– *Genesis 30:43.*

Jacob would not have been this wealthy if he still depended on Laban. It was what Jacob had to offer Laban that brought wealth to Laban. But how was Jacob able to come up with something to offer Laban after so many years of slaving under Laban?

Jacob's offer to Laban was a well thought out offer. Jacob's offer to Laban was not a guess work. When Laban offered Jacob more wages, Jacob did not have to go and think about it. Jacob was prepared for every possibility and every eventuality with Laban.

THE PROCESS

Over time as Jacob's family grew, Jacob's income could no longer take care of his family. Tension and complains were setting into Jacob's family and gradually becoming the order. Jacob's dream for his family with his present income was no longer possible. All these concerns got Jacob thinking. All these family demands weighed heavily on Jacob's mind.

Jacob knew that he could no longer stay the way he was. Coping was no longer going to be possible if he continued like this. There was a very deep dissatisfaction in Jacob over his finance and affairs as against his growing responsibilities over his family. Sleepless nights became regular with Jacob.

ENGAGE YOUR MIND

Jacob's mind became seriously engaged everyday on a possible way out. Then one day, as Jacob's mind was engaged on a possible way out, an idea hit him. Jacob was able to stop depending on Laban and rather offer Laban something because he engaged his mind. Jacob put his mind to work.

Your wealth is a product of what you have to offer. And what you have to offer is a product of what your mind can offer. What you have to offer is principally a product of what your mind can produce.

A WORKING MIND IS A WORKING LIFE

Engaging your mind productively opens you up to a variety of things you can offer your generation. Putting your mind to work naturally gives you work. You can't be idle if your mind is productively engaged. You can't be looking for where to work or what to do if your mind is working.

The reason why many are not working (complaining that there are no jobs) is because their minds are not working. The reason why many are idle is because their minds are idle. Idle hands are products of idle minds.

You don't need to apply for a job anywhere before you start working. All you truly need to start working is to put your mind to work. All you really need to get a job is to engage your mind. This why we go to school. This why we get educated.

THE ILLITERATES OF THIS AGE

The major reason for school and education is not just get accepted by people and fit into the society with all manners of accreditations and certifications piled up to your credit-which is not bad. But beyond that, of what use are your certificates if you are still frustrated and stranded in life?

The primary and sole aim of schooling and getting an education should be to teach and to show you how to use your mind productively. The true purpose of getting educated is to train your mind to harness the opportunities around you. The real purpose of education is development.

The true purpose of education should be to train and develop your mind to better your life. Training and developing the mind should be the major focus of education. If this is the case, then, no one who has ever passed through school or gotten an education should have any reason to complain or become stranded or frustrated in life.

THE MAIN FOCUS

Therefore, the illiterates of this generation are not those who did not go to school neither are they those without the supposed traditional sense of education and certifications. Rather the illiterates of these times are those whose minds are not tapped and developed. Those whose minds are trapped.

Those whose minds are myopic and threatened; those whose minds are blind; those whose minds refuse change and innovation; those whose minds fold when squeezed by change and times-these are the real illiterates of our times. They may have the certificates. They may have all the formalities. But they are not really educated. Education goes beyond formalities.

This is why if you are frustrated and stranded in life despite all your certificates and years in school then you were never educated. You only went through school; the school did not go through you. It is one thing to go through school and it is yet another thing for the school to go through you.

WHO IS TO BLAME

So many have gone through school but the school did not go through them. This is the bane of so many in our society today. Real education lies not just in going to school but in allowing the school to go through you. It is this two-edged process that makes for real education. It is this two-edged process that springs up development.

This is why, real education lies in the development and total transformation of the mind. The lack of jobs and unemployment in our world today only shows the level of mental degradation at work in the lives of so many. The lack of jobs only shows the lack of minds at work.

Unemployment is not just a problem of the government or the economy or the private institutions. Unemployment is a core problem of the mind.

Unemployment is a personal problem and not a general problem. It is not a problem of the government but a problem of the mind. Unemployment is a shame on the mind.

MINE YOUR MIND

If you are unemployed then your unemployment is a big shame on your mind. If you don't have a job then your joblessness is a shame on your mind. We are in a time where many are so mentally lazy. They want things done for them. They want ready made things-ready made jobs-ready made homes-ready made opportunities-ready made offices-ready made wealth-ready made everything.

They don't want to work out anything instead they want things worked out for them. Life is not colored or patterned that way. If your mind is not working, you are wasting. And if your mind is working, you will not have any reason to complain or be frustrated in life. Your life's worth is in your mind's work. Watch it! If your mind is working, you will naturally be working.

For you to have something to offer, your mind must go to work. What you can offer lies in what your mind can offer. Poverty is simply the neglect of the mind. When the mind is neglected, poverty is generated.

Look at Lazarus.

He sat to beg everyday from the same man. His only desire was to beg.

> *"And there was a certain beggar*
> *named Lazarus, which was laid*
> *at his gate, full of sores,*
>
> *And desiring to be fed with the crumbs*
> *which fell from the rich man's table . . . "*
>
> *– Luke 16:20-21.*

Lazarus had a faulty mind. Lazarus had a begging mind. Lazarus had a dead mind. All Lazarus could think of everyday was to beg. Begging was the only thing that occupied Lazarus' mind. Lazarus could not think of anything else aside from begging. How can a man think of nothing else but begging?

YOUR MIND IS THE KEY

Lazarus could not use his mind. Lazarus could not productively engage his mind. What a loss! What a pity! What a shame! Poverty is a product of a dead mind. Until your mind becomes active, your life will remain passive. Until your mind comes alive, your life will not come alive.

Until your mind begins to work, your life will not work. Lazarus was a beggar not because of his condition or situation which is not particular but rather Lazarus was a beggar because of his mind. Lazarus had a begging life because he had a begging mind. Lazarus was poor because his mind was poor.

Begging was the only thing on Lazarus' mind. Lazarus had no information and did not bother to seek for any information to better his life. Everyday he just sat down at the gate to beg.

THE REAL POVERTY

No man can escape the reality of his mind. Whatever is real in your mind becomes real in your life. The reality of life begins from the mind. When poverty is entrenched in the mind of a man, that man naturally comes under the evil grip of poverty.

The poverty of the mind is the worst kind of poverty. When a mind is poor, its life will also be poor. Everyone is essentially a core product of their minds. Everyone is a function of their minds. Everyone is a candid reflection of their minds.

One-day Jesus gave a parable about a sower as he taught the multitude.

> *"A sower went out to sow his seed:*
> *and as he sowed, some fell by the way side:*
> *and it was trodden down, and the*
> *fowls of the air devoured it.*

> *And some fell upon a rock; and as it*
> *sprung up, it withered away, because it lacked moisture.*
>
> *And some fell among the thorns;*
> *and the thorns sprang up with it, and choked it.*
>
> *And other fell on the good ground, and*
> *sprang up, and bare fruit an hundred fold . . . "*
>
> *– Luke 8:5-8.*

This sower sowed seeds on different grounds-the wayside, the rock, the thorns and the good ground. These four different grounds all received the same seeds. But out of all the four grounds, only one ground brought forth fruits. Of all four grounds, only one ground produced fruits. Why did the other grounds not produce fruits?

Why was it only the good ground that produced fruits; after all, it was the same seeds that were sown on all four grounds? The problem was not with the seeds because the same seeds that did not produce on the other grounds produced on the good ground. The problem was with the grounds.

The reason why despite the fact that seeds entered those grounds and they still did not produce fruits was because of the kind of grounds that those grounds were. And so if a million seeds were pumped into those grounds they will still not produce fruits.

When Jesus was interpreting the parable of the sower to his disciples, He interpreted the ground to be the heart or the mind of men.

> *"Now the parable is this:*
> *The seed is the word of God.*
>
> *Those by the way side are they*
> *that hear then cometh the devil, and*
> *taketh away the word out of their hearts,*
> *lest they should believe and be saved . . .*

But that on the good ground are they,
which in an honest and good heart,
having heard the word, keep it and bring
forth fruit with patience."

– Luke 8:11-12, 15.

The book of Matthew gives us a clearer picture.

"Hear ye therefore
the parable of the sower.

When any one heareth the word
of the kingdom, and understandeth it not,
then cometh the wicked one, and catcheth
away that which was sown in his heart.
This is he which receiveth seed by the wayside."

– Matthew 13:18-19.

The ground is the heart or the mind in contemporary language. Nothing determines your life like your mind. Nothing determines your destiny like your mind. The kind of mind you have is what determines the kind of life you will have. You are what you are because of the kind of mind you have.

IF YOUR MIND CAN CATCH IT

You are where you are because of the kind of mind you have. The problem was not with the seed. The problem was with the mind. The reason why fruits failed to manifest was because of the kind of mind (ground) in question.

If you think you are a failure, it is principally because your mind is a failure. If you think you are poor, it is essentially because your mind is poor. If you think you are down then it is because your mind is down. Poverty is a product of the mind. Failure is a product of the mind.

Poor minds produce poor lives. Wherever you see poverty, you also see poor minds. The poverty of any life is purely a product of the poverty of the mind. This is why poverty is internal and not external. Failure is internal and not external. Before a man becomes wealthy outside, he must first of all become wealthy inside.

Before a man fails outside, he would have failed inside. Before a man is poor outside, he would have been poor inside. The inside of a man is far more important than the outside of a man.

WEALTH IS INTERNAL BEFORE IT'S EXTERNAL

The inside of a man is what determines the outside of a man. The inside of a man is what shapes the outside of a man. Whatever you are outside is what you have already become inside. Inside is what moulds outside. This is why for anyone to conquer poverty outside; that person must first of all conquer poverty inside.

> *"Beloved, I wish above all things*
> *that thou mayest prosper and be in health,*
> *even as thy soul prospereth."*
>
> *– 3rd John 2.*

Your prosperity outside is according to your prosperity inside. Your wealth outside is according to your wealth inside. You can't be wealthy inside and be poor outside. And you can't be poor inside and be wealthy outside. Until you prosper inside, you can't prosper outside. This is why it takes a wealthy mind to have a wealthy life. It takes a rich mind to have a rich life.

It takes a successful mind to have a successful life. If you must produce outside then you must produce inside. The first step to enriching your life is enriching your mind. A poor mind can never have a rich life. Your mind is your wealth mine. Your mind is your wealth. The true measure of a man's wealth is not in his external possessions but in his internal possessions.

It is what you possess inside you that truly measures your wealth. What you carry inside is what determines what you will possess outside. What you carry inside is what produces what you will carry outside. Nothing measures your wealth like what you carry inside. Nothing determines your wealth like what you possess inside.

YOUR CONTENT MATTERS

The wealthy pay attention to what they possess inside than what they possess outside and that is because what you possess inside is what determines what you possess outside. Internal possessions are what determines external possessions. Without internal possessions, there will be no external possessions.

This is why your wealth is a product of your internal possessions. It is what you carry inside that gives you access to wealth outside. Wealth answers to what you carry inside. You must carry something inside if you must access wealth outside. If you carry nothing inside you will have nothing outside.

EMPTINESS IS NOT AN OPTION

Wealth is not for those who are empty inside. Wealth is for those who are loaded inside. Wealth is not for those who carry nothing inside. Wealth is for those who carry something inside. Wealth is not for empty barrels. You can't be empty inside and be loaded outside. Neither can you be loaded inside and be empty outside.

The difference between the wealthy and the poor is what they carry inside. What you carry inside is what really makes the difference outside. Make no mistake: wealth answers to what you carry inside. Wealth answers to content. If you carry nothing inside, wealth has nothing to answer to.

Look at Lazarus and the rich man. Lazarus was so poor and the rich man was so rich. Lazarus had poverty and the rich man had wealth. When Lazarus and the rich man died, the secrets behind the wealth and poverty of the rich man and Lazarus were revealed.

> *"But Abraham said, Son, remember*
> *that thou in thy lifetime receivedst*
> *thy good things and likewise Lazarus evil things . . ."*
>
> *– Luke 16:25.*

The rich man was rich because of the good things he received. And Lazarus was poor because of the evil things he received. The difference between the rich man and Lazarus was in what they received. The difference between the rich man and Lazarus was in their content.

WHAT IS INSIDE YOU

What the rich man carried inside was different from what Lazarus carried inside. Content was the major difference between the rich man and Lazarus. Content was what separated Lazarus from the rich man. Content was what made the rich man rich and Lazarus poor.

Nothing separates the rich from the poor like content. Nothing differentiates the rich from the poor like content. Content is what makes the difference in the life of anyone. What essentially makes anyone rich or poor is content. Content is what determines people.

Content is what separates people. Everyone is a product of their content. The kind of content you have is what determines the kind of life you will have.

A CHANGE IS NEEDED

Lazarus was poor because of the kind of content he had. Poverty is a product of a bad content. Poverty is product of poor content. Poverty is a product of wrong content. As such, poverty shows the need for a new content. Poverty shows the need for a change in content. Until a man's content changes, a man's life will not change.

Until something changes in you nothing can change for you. You can't have the same content and have a different result. Lazarus was poor because he had a poor mind. And because Lazarus had a poor mind, Lazarus could not put his mind to work. Lazarus could not engage his mind productively because he had a poor mind.

Lazarus' mind was inactive because his mind was poor. And because Lazarus did not use his mind which was as a result of the poverty of his mind, he did not have anything to offer to anyone.

ENRICH YOUR MIND

No mind can work or function in poverty. A poor mind can never be productive. Productivity begins with empowerment-mental empowerment. Productivity begins with enrichment. For you to put your mind to work, your mind must be enriched; your mind must be empowered. The reason why a lot of minds cannot work is because a lot of minds are poor.

The reason why many cannot productively engage their mind is because their minds are poor. It takes a rich mind to have an active mind. Until you enrich your mind you can't engage your mind. For your mind to be productively engaged, your mind has to be deliberately enriched; your mind has to be loaded. And knowledge is what enriches the mind.

KNOWLEDGE IS WEALTH

Knowledge is what makes the mind rich. Knowledge is the wealth of the mind. A mind is poor because it lacks knowledge. A mind is poor because it does not have knowledge. The poverty of the mind is actually the poverty of knowledge. For your mind to be rich, your mind must be filled with knowledge.

Until your mind is filled with knowledge, your mind cannot be put to productive use. It is like trying to drive a car without fuel. It will move let alone drive. Whatsoever fuel is to a car, that is what knowledge is to the mind. Knowledge is what drives the mind to produce. For your mind to work effectively, your mind needs knowledge.

Knowledge is the key of the mind. Knowledge is what drives the mind to work. Knowledge is what makes the mind productive. Productivity is a function of knowledge. Productivity is an offspring of knowledge. Only a mind soaked with knowledge can produce results. This is why the first step towards having a productive mind is to pursue knowledge.

The first step towards having an active mind is to go after knowledge. Without knowledge, the mind cannot function. Without knowledge, the mind grows dull and eventually becomes dead.

YOUR MIND NEEDS KNOWLEDGE

Your mind cannot survive without knowledge. Knowledge makes the mind sharp. An active mind is a mind loaded with knowledge. A working mind is a mind soaked with knowledge. When your mind begins to work, your life begins to have varieties of things to offer to men.

Jacob was able to come up with an offer for Laban because he engaged his mind. And Jacob was able to engage his mind because he had vast knowledge of sheep, cattle and goats; animal husbandry. All along, before Jacob came up with an offer for Laban, Jacob was just working with his hands and not with his mind.

MINDS BEFORE HANDS

While Jacob was just working with his hands, he could not cater for his family; he was struggling to survive; he was poor. But when Jacob started working with his mind as he worked with his hands, there was a paradigm shift. Jacob who was poor was now so rich. Jacob who had nothing now had all things.

A combination of working with his mind and working with his hands brought Jacob great wealth. Wealth is a combination of working hands and working minds. Wealth is a combination of hand work and mind work. Wealth is a product of the work of your hands and the work of your mind.

Your mind as well as your hands must work if your wealth must come. Wealth is totally impossible without the work of the mind. Your mind must be engaged for your wealth to emerge. A lot of people are just concerned about their physical work and nothing more.

Without the working of your mind, your wealth will remain impossible. It is the effect of the mind that puts wealth within your reach. It is the touch of the mind that gives you access to wealth. Your mind must go to work just as your hands go to work.

JOURNEY TO WEALTH

WEALTH IS FUNDAMENTALLY A PERSONAL CHOICE

BY: JOSHUA GREAT

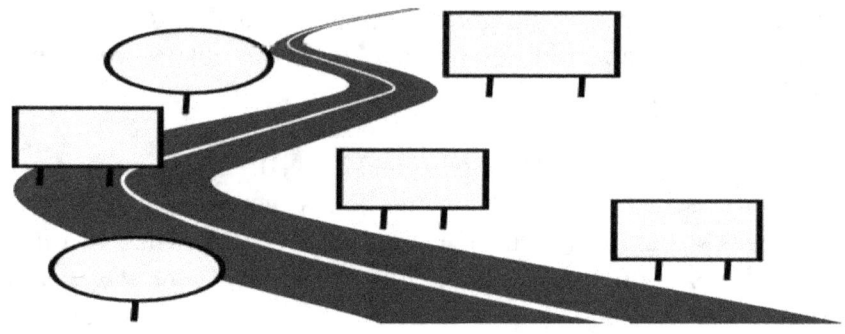

CHAPTER FOUR
IT IS NOT NATURAL

As the global famine continued, Egypt grew richer; Egypt grew wealthier. Every other person, every other nation, every other tribe decreased while Egypt increased. Egypt's increase was steady and sure. As long as the famine prevailed, Egypt was sure of great increase.

Egypt's increase was as sure as the day. More so, the reason Egypt increased and grew in wealth was because Egypt had something to offer to the world. Egypt had answers to the problems of the world. And that afforded Egypt the opportunity of unimaginable dimensions of wealth.

Egypt had something to offer the world not because they were lucky nor did they guess their way to the solution of the world; what Egypt had to offer was a product of revelation. Under the great leadership of Joseph, a covenant man of destiny, Egypt was able to solve the problem of the world because there was a revelation.

> *"And it came to pass at the end*
> *of two full years, that Pharaoh dreamed:*
> *and, behold, he stood by the river.*
> *And, behold, there came up out of the river,*
> *seven well favoured kine and fatfleshed;*
> *and they fed in a meadow.*
>
> *And, behold, seven other kine came up*
> *after them out of the river; ill favored and*
> *leanfleshed; and stood by the other kine*
> *upon the brink of the river.*
>
> *And the ill favored and leanfleshed*
> *kine did eat up the seven well favored and fat kine.*
> *So Pharaoh awoke.*
>
> *And he slept and dreamed the second time:*

*and, behold, seven ears of corn came
up upon one stalk, rank and good.*

*And, behold, seven thin ears and blasted
with the east wind sprung up after them.*

*And the seven thin ears devoured the
seven rank and full ears. And Pharaoh awoke,
and, behold, it was a dream."*

– Genesis 41:1-7.

It was this dream of Pharaoh, king of Egypt that brought about the revelation of the famine. It was the revelation of the famine that gave Egypt the privilege of having something to offer to the world. It was the revelation of the famine that gave Egypt answers to the problems of the world.

ACCESS ANSWERS

If Egypt did not have that revelation, Egypt would have ended up as a victim like everyone else. But revelation gave Egypt something to offer. Nothing gives you something to offer your generation like revelations. Nothing gives you answers to problems of men like revelations.

Nothing gives you access to the solutions of men like revelations. And nothing gives you access to unhindered wealth like having answers to the problems of men. Your access to the answers of men's questions lies in your access to revelations. Your access to the solutions of men's problems lies in your access to revelations. Revelation opens you up to answers.

Revelation connects you to solutions. For you to be a solution provider which is your sure access to wealth, you must be a revelation receiver. You need to receive revelations if you must possess solutions. Solutions answers to revelations. Solutions are products of revelations.

When Sarah could not yet give birth to a son, Sarah decided to have children for her husband Abraham through her servant, bearing in mind that every child born from her servant for her husband, could still be called her own since her servant had her blessing to be with her husband. This was Sarah's way of consoling herself over her inability to bear children yet.

> *"Now Sarai Abram's wife bare him no children:*
> *and she had an handmaid, an Egyptian,*
> *whose name was Hagar.*
>
> *And Sarai said unto Abram, Behold now,*
> *the LORD hath restrained me from bearing:*
> *I pray thee, go in unto my maid; it may be*
> *that I may obtain children by her. And Abram*
> *hearkened to the voice of Sarai.*
>
> *And Sarai Abram's wife took Hagar*
> *her maid, the Egyptian, after Abram hath*
> *dwelt ten years in the land of Canaan, and*
> *gave her to her husband Abram to be his wife."*
>
> *– Genesis 16:1-3.*

Hagar became pregnant and eventually gave birth to a son for Abraham. And he was named Ishmael. In the process of time, God also visited Sarah and she also gave birth to a son and he was named Isaac. Both sons continued to grow under Abraham their father. But Hagar and her son took pleasure in mocking Sarah and her son. And as a result Hagar and her son were sent packing.

As Hagar left with her son, they wondered in the wilderness where they exhausted every food and drink they had. With no food and especially no water, Hagar prepared for the worst–death. In her helplessness, Hagar abandoned her son to his fate in the wilderness expecting the worst to happen. But something miraculous happened.

> *"And the water was spent in the bottle,*
> *and she cast the child under one of the shrubs.*
>
> *And she went, and sat her down over*

> *against him a good way off, as it were a bowshot: for she said, let me not see the death of the child. And she sat over against him and lift up her voice and wept.*
>
> *And God heard the voice of the lad: and the angel of God called to Hagar out of heaven, and said unto her, what aileth thee, Hagar? Fear not, for God hath heard the voice of the lad, where he is.*
>
> *Arise, lift up the lad and hold him in thy hand: for I will make him a great nation.*
>
> *And God opened her eyes, and she saw a well of water: and she went, and filled the bottle with water, and gave the lad drink."*
>
> *– Genesis 21:15-19.*

Hagar was looking for answers. Hagar was looking for a solution. Hagar was looking for water. And yet despite her desperate search, she could not get water. Despite her desperate search, she could not have a solution. She tried her best but her best could not give her rest. And when she realized that her ability was actually her inability, she resigned to fate.

In the midst of Hagar's helplessness, God opened her eyes. In the midst of her helplessness, God gave her a revelation. All of a sudden her eyes were opened to a well of water. All along this well of water was around the corner; not far away; but Hagar could not see it. Her solution was just around her but her natural eyes could not catch it.

SEE WHAT OTHERS DON'T SEE
It was not until her eyes were opened before she could see the solution she was looking for. Most times the answers we seek are beyond the reach of our natural eyes and understanding. Most times the answers we seek are just around us but we seem not to be able to see them. This is where

revelation comes in. Revelation help you see what you naturally cannot see.

Revelation helps you to catch what you naturally cannot catch. Revelation gives you an edge. Revelation helps you access what you naturally cannot access. Revelation helps you beyond the natural.

Most of the problems in the world today are not ordinary. Most of the situations of men today are not natural. As such the solutions to match these problems cannot be anything ordinary or natural. This is why revelation is needful in our time.

JOURNEY TO WEALTH

WEALTH IS FUNDAMENTALLY A PERSONAL CHOICE

BY: JOSHUA GREAT

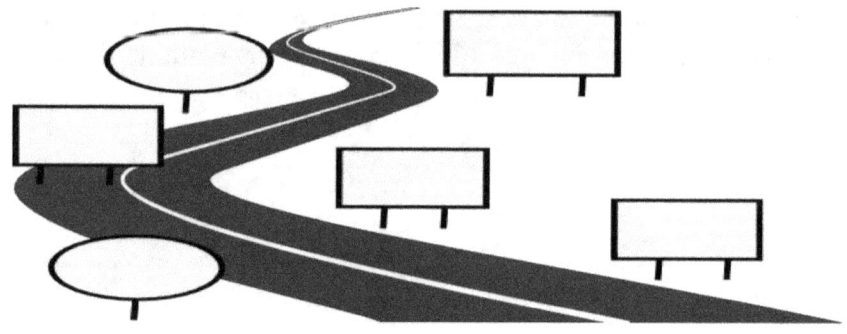

CHAPTER FIVE
TAP INTO IT

Egypt became wealthy because everyone and every nation gave their money, substance and possession to Egypt in exchange for food.

> *"And all countries came into Egypt to Joseph for to buy corn; because that the famine was sore in all lands."*
>
> *– Genesis 41:57.*

You can imagine the traffic of wealth into Egypt on a daily basis as every country in the world marched through her boarders for food. Unimaginable dimensions of wealth from the coffers of nations was transferred to Egypt. The wealth of Egypt was a product of a massive wealth transfer.

Egypt emerged so wealthy because wealth was heavily transferred to Egypt. Egypt enjoyed wealth transfer. The cheapest way to become wealthy especially in these last days is to tap into the massive flow of wealth transfer. Wealth is constantly being transferred on a regular basis.

Wealth is constantly moving from hand to hand. Wealth is constantly seeking new grounds and new lives. Your ability to tap into the regular busy traffic of wealth is what gives you access to wealth. You need to position yourself for wealth transfer. You need to access the flow of wealth transfer.

Job who lost everything was able to become rich again because wealth was transferred to him.

> *" . . . every man also gave him a piece of money, and every one an earring of gold."*
>
> *- Job 42:1*

You can imagine everyone giving you money. Job was able to access wealth again by wealth transfer. And God is still in the business of transferring wealth to people. God is still giving people access to the flow of wealth.

All along Jacob had been struggling in poverty until he got caught up in the flow of wealth transfer. The wealth of Laban was transferred to Jacob. Jacob who had nothing now had everything and Laban who had everything now had nothing.

> *"And the man increased exceedingly, and had much cattle . . . , and camels, and asses.*
>
> *And He heard the words of Laban's sons saying, Jacob hath taken away all that was our father's; and of that which was our father's hath he gotten all this glory."*
>
> *– Genesis 30:43; 31:1.*

Every wealth Laban had was transferred to Jacob. Every glory Laban had was transferred to Jacob. Every possession Laban had was transferred to Jacob. Money is always changing hands. Wealth is always changing hands and because wealth is always changing hands, wealth is very slippery in nature. This is why wealth demands caution.

With wealth comes caution. With success comes caution. With money comes caution. Without caution you will lose money. Without caution you will lose wealth. Without caution, you can't get wealth. If you are not careful, life will be painful. If you are not careful, wealth will slip away and may never surface again. It is very easy to fail. It is very easy to be poor.

To come down is very easy. What is not easy, is to climb up. What is not easy, is to succeed. What is not easy, is wealth. Wealth is very slippery. As such, caution is your grip on wealth. Caution is your grip on money. One of the fundamental things you must learn as you ascend the ladder of wealth is caution. You must learn caution. You must learn to be careful whether you like it or not.

YOUR PORTION IS IN YOUR CAUTION

Life will naturally teach you caution. And until you have been taught; not necessarily by men or institutions but by life, which is the place of experience, you don't really stand a chance. If you must gather money, you must first learn to be cautious. If you must access wealth, you must first learn to be careful.

Wealth and caution go together. Wealth and caution are so connected together. One cannot be without the other. Those who are truly wealthy are extremely careful. Even in their daring moves or ventures, they are still extremely careful. In fact, the higher they go, the more careful they are. New heights require new caution. Caution is one major characters of wealth.

IT CAN DISAPPEAR

Just like Laban, so many who had it yesterday, no longer have it today. Only very few who had it yesterday still have it today. So many are basking in the glories of yester-years. There is nothing fresh in them. There is nothing new about them. There is nothing to write home about today. Their lives are full of old stuffs; old victories, old successes. Nothing new is happening.

So many who use to have it have missed it. They no longer have it. This is the mysterious fluidity of life. Money has no permanent residence. Wealth has no permanent landlord. Wealth is always flowing and only those who tap into its flow become beneficiaries of its bounties.

If you misbehave with wealth, you will miss wealth. That is why with wealth, caution is not a choice but a must and with caution comes discipline.

> *"... for riches certainly make themselves wings;*
> *they fly away as an eagle toward heaven."*
>
> *– Proverbs 23:5.*

So many who were wealthy in the past, are now paupers in the present. So many who had abundance in the past are now beggars today. Some of the poor you see today were once very rich. Wealth is very fluid in nature. Wealth is a flow. Wealth is not something you have and just relax. No! To relax is to regret.

Just as wealth can flow into your life, wealth can also flow out of your life. This is why wealth warrants a lot of caution. It is so easy to become poor but not so easy to become rich. If wealth was easy, everybody would be wealthy. Accessing wealth is an uphill task. Accessing wealth is a big challenge.

THE FLUID NATURE
Job was the wealthiest man in his days. No one was as rich as Job. The wealth of Job was so vast and incredibly massive.

> *"His substance also was seven thousand sheep,*
> *and three thousand camels, and*
> *five hundred yoke of oxen, and*
> *five hundred she asses, and a very great household;*
> *so that this man was the greatest of all the men of the east."*
>
> *– Job 1:3.*

The dimension of Job's wealth was unimaginably monumental. But despite the massive wealth of Job, Job lost all the wealth he had. From being the richest, Job became the poorest. If Job, despite his wealth could still become poor, even though he became rich again, then there is no one alive today who cannot become poor no matter how rich he or she may be.

Listen to this;

> *"And saying, Alas, alas, that great city,*
> *that was clothed in fine linen, and purple,*
> *and scarlet, and decked with gold,*
> *and precious stones, and pearls!*

For in one hour so great riches is come to nought,
And every shipmaster, and all the company in ships,
and sailors, and as many as trade by sea, stood afar off

And cried when they saw the smoke of her
burning, saying, What city is like this great city!

And they cast dust on their heads, and cried,
weeping and wailing, saying, Alas, alas that
great city, wherein were made rich all that had
ships in the sea by reason of her costliness!
for in one hour is she made desolate."

– Revelations 18:16-19

Here lies a story showing the twist of fate upon a city thought to be so indestructible. It is totally impossible to think or believe that a city with so much greatness and unimaginable dimensions of wealth can be reduced to nothing within one hour.

One hour is grossly unthinkable for a city with such great wealth to come to nothing. Everything that made that city great; everything that made that city rich and thick; everything that made that city the envy of men, all perished within one hour. There is no one who has anything anywhere today, who cannot lose it tomorrow.

LIVE CAREFULLY

There is nothing that anyone has today that cannot be gone or lost tomorrow. If it happened to Job, then it can happen to anyone. This is the more reason why you should be careful. You should tread with caution. Live carefully-that is the best way to live.

Anything can be lost. Anything can go. That is the blunt reality of life. To ignore this reality is to deceive yourself and setup yourself for your own peril and downfall; of which so many have already done. So many have shot themselves in their legs. This is the sorry reason behind the pathetic situations of many.

The downfall of many is that they think that what they have managed to have or secure can guarantee their tomorrow. With this thought, many exude unfounded confidence that tends to ignore caution. The confidence that ignores caution is foolishness.

TOMORROW IS A MYSTERY

It is in man not to be able to predict his ways. This is the unfortunate reality that befalls humanity. The inability to see, know or predict tomorrow, is the grave limitation that perpetually plagues and haunts our human existence. We long to know what will happen but we cannot. That knowledge is beyond our reach. All we can ever know is what is happening or what has happened.

The knowledge of tomorrow is way beyond our league. Tomorrow is a mystery. Tomorrow is totally unknown and the unknown should breed caution. The unknown should not scare you but should make you careful; not too careful though because anyone who is too careful will gradually become fearful.

History is full of men who had massive wealth but ended up miserable in poverty. History is full of men who had great means who later ended up with no means. History is full of men who thought they had it only for them to discover that they no longer have it. Just as tomorrow is a mystery, wealth is also a mystery; a mystery that still eludes the general understanding of so many.

Wealth is something that if you think you have it you will lose it. Wealth is something that even if you have it you must act as if you don't have it. In other words your wealth must not or never enter your head. Your trust must never be in your wealth. If it does it will be gone before you even know it.

WEALTH CAN BLIND

The unfounded confidence in wealth is the alluring deception of wealth. Wealth will always deceive those who put their trust and confidence in it. Having it and thinking that you have it only prepares you to lose it. The confidence in wealth only makes a man blind while it leads him to destruction.

Wealth can make a man blind and can be grossly misleading. That is why the confidence of wealth has made many to lose their wealth. The confidence of wealth is what has reduced so many to poverty. Never put your confidence in any wealth or substance. The deception of wealth is real and the reality of that deception is destruction.

Listen to this;

"... if riches increase, set not your heart upon them."

– Psalms 62:10.

" He that trusteth in his riches shall fall ... "

– Proverbs 11:28.

Those who make wealth their confidence always have bitter stories to tell. Laban would never have believed that Jacob who was his servant, could ever rise far above him. When Laban consented to Jacob's idea, he had so much confidence in his wealth and possessions. He could not see a shift coming over his supposed wealth.

Look at the confidence of Laban.

"And Laban said, Behold, I would it might be according to thy word."

– Genesis 30:34.

What a confidence Laban displayed. But Laban's confidence in his wealth and possessions failed him. Laban lost everything to Jacob. Wealth was transferred away from Laban to Jacob. From time immemorial, from generation to generation, from age to age, from dispensation to dispensation, from nation to nation, wealth has always been a thing of transfer. Wealth is always a transfer. Wealth is always seeking for points and places of transfer.

THE FLOW IS ON

Wealth is transference in nature; where those who have it seek to keep it and those who don't have it seek to have it. Wealth is constantly changing hands and places. And the easiest way to become wealthy is to tap into the flow of wealth transfer; becoming a recipient of wealth transfer. Wealth is always moving around. You need to position yourself for wealth to locate you.

There are certain things that positions a man for wealth transfer. Massive wealth is always on the move. Massive wealth is always and constantly being transferred from one place to another, from one life to another, from one hand to another. Your life can be the next point for the transfer of wealth. Your life can attract the next flow of wealth transfer. The flow of wealth can be directed to you. But certain things must be in place for you to enjoy the flow of wealth.

(1) RIGHTEOUSNESS

"... the wealth of the sinner is laid up for the just."

– Proverbs 13:22.

Nothing gives you access to the transfer of wealth like righteousness. Nothing directs wealth to flow in your direction like righteousness. Nothing commands the flow of wealth into your life like righteousness. Righteousness positions you for wealth transfer. Righteousness opens you up to wealth transfer.

Righteousness is your sure access to the transfer of wealth. Your key to the flow of wealth is righteousness. In the grand scheme of things, righteousness is the foundation for wealth. For you to enjoy wealth transfer, you must embrace righteousness.

SELECTIVE BY NATURE

The transfer of wealth is not for everybody. Only those who stand in righteousness can tap into the flow of wealth. Wealth is a mystery. And only God who is the source of wealth can decode the mystery behind wealth. God in His wisdom shows that righteousness is the sure path to lasting wealth.

Wealth is always flowing. Wealth is always constantly moving. Just as wealth is moving away from someone, wealth is moving towards someone. Just as wealth is transferred away from someone, wealth is transferred to someone.

" Wealth gotten by vanity shall be diminished . . . "

– Proverbs 13:11.

Every wealth gotten by unrighteous practice automatically moves wealth away. Wealth flows away from unrighteousness. You don't have to cheat to become rich. You don't have to lie to make it. You don't have to dupe or deceive anyone to become wealthy. You don't have to kill to become rich.

You don't need any form of unrighteousness to become wealthy. Any form of unrighteousness automatically disqualifies you from accessing true wealth - wealth with peace of mind - wealth with a clear conscience.

THE MYSTERY

Two houses were built at about the same time. One was built on a foundation of sand and the other was built on a rock foundation. In the process of time, the house with the foundation of sand collapsed while the house with the rock foundation remained standing.

*" Therefore whosoever heareth these
sayings of mine, and doeth them, I will liken
him unto a wise man, which built his house upon a rock:*

*And the rain descended, and the floods came,
and the winds blew, and beat upon that house;
and it fell not for it was founded upon a rock.*

*And everyone that heareth these sayings of mine,
and doeth them not, shall be likened unto a*

foolish man, which built his upon the sand:

And the rain descended and the floods came, and the winds blew, and beat upon that house; and it fell: and great was the fall of it."

– Matthew 7:24-27.

Every wealth gotten through any form of unrighteousness is like the foolish man who built his house upon the sand. It may appear to be but its only for a while. It will not last, it will surely fall. When unrighteousness becomes the foundation of your wealth, your wealth becomes doomed for failure.

Just like the house built on the sand that appears to be but is not, instead collapsed and perished, so is every wealth gotten through unrighteousness. It may appear for a while; its only for a while. It may appear to endure; it may appear to last but it will so disappear sooner than it appeared.

WELLS WITHOUT WATER

Every wealth gotten through any form of unrighteousness only has an appearance with no lasting assurance. Of what use is an appearance without an assurance? It is better not to have tasted wealth than for you to taste it and lose it.

You can imagine a building like a skyscraper collapsing with people inside. The people inside the collapsed building will end up dead and if there is any chance of survival, those who survive will be fatally injured. In like manner, not only will every wealth gotten through unrighteousness perish but those who access such dirty wealth will end up so afflicted and so destroyed.

With such results, what is the use of getting wealth through unrighteousness? Is it not foolishness to build what you know will collapse? Is it not foolishness to go after something you now know will not last? Is it not foolishness to pursue what will end up as a colossal waste? Is it not foolishness to engage in what will only end up becoming useless?

SOMETHING MORE IMPORTANT

What is dirty is harmful. If your wealth is dirty then your wealth is harmful. Just as it is gross foolishness to build a house on sand, it is equally gross foolishness to pursue wealth through unrighteous means. Wealth through unrighteousness is only a display of foolishness even though many may think its smartness or wisdom.

Just like building a house on sand only ends up as a waste, in like manner, every wealth built through unrighteousness will only end up as a waste. Every wealth gotten through unrighteousness will only end up becoming useless. Don't be fooled. Don't end up as a waste. Don't end up becoming useless. Don't end up losing your relevance.

Those who think that they are wise, always end up displaying their foolishness to their shame, at the glare of everybody. There is no wisdom in any form of unrighteousness. Foolishness is always the end of every form of unrighteousness.

God told Joshua;

"This book of the law shall not depart out of thy mouth: but thou shalt meditate therein day and night, that thou mayest observe to do according to all that is written therein; for then thou shalt make thy way prosperous, and then thou shall have good success."

– Joshua 1:8

It is not every success that is good. It is not every money that is good. It is not every wealth that is good. There is good success and there is bad success. There is good money and there is bad money. There is good wealth and there is bad wealth. Good wealth is wealth gotten through good means. And bad wealth is wealth gotten through bad means.

Wealth in itself is not bad. It is the means by which it is gotten that makes it either good or bad. The definition is in the means. The determining factor is in the means. True wealth is defined by its means. Any wealth gotten without a clear conscience is a bad wealth. And bad wealth is lost wealth.

Bad wealth is no wealth. Bad wealth is fake wealth. Every wealth gotten through wrong means has no future. Every wealth gotten through wrong means will surely depart.

IT EITHER FLOWS OR DRIES

Every wealth gotten through evil means will surely fade away. Wealth does not stay with you because you got it. Wealth stays with you because of how you got it. How you get your wealth is what determines if wealth will stay with you or not.

Your grip over wealth lies in your means to wealth. Whether wealth will flow away from you or flow towards you, your means is what will determine it. Your means to wealth is what determines if wealth will move away from you or not. Wealth stays or moves by means. Wealth flows or dries by means. Wealth is attracted or diverted by means.

If wealth is going to stay with you then your means is what will determine it. Any wrong means to wealth always moves wealth away. Any wrong means to wealth transfers wealth away. Nothing dispossesses a man from wealth like wrong means.

YOUR MEANS MUST BE RIGHT

Nothing disconnects a man from wealth like wrong means. If your means to wealth is wrong then the wealth you seek will not stay. Any means to wealth other than righteousness is a means in vain. Your means to wealth is what determines your future with wealth.

Listen! Your means to wealth is far more important than the wealth you seek. Your means is what determines your future. Your means is what holds your future. No matter how wealthy a man is, if the means to his wealth is wrong, the wealth will depart. Wealth does not stay with evil. Wealth cannot stay without righteousness.

Look at David.

*"Truly God is good to Israel,
even to such as are of a clean heart.*

*But as for me, my feet were almost gone;
my steps hath well nigh slipped.*

*For I was envious at the foolish,
when I saw the prosperity of the wicked.*

*For there are no bands in their death:
but their strength is firm.*

*They are not in trouble as other men;
neither are they plagued like other men.*

*Therefore pride compasseth them as a chain;
violence covereth them as a garment.*

*Their eyes stand out with fatness;
they have more than heart could wish.*

*They are corrupt, and speak wickedly
concerning oppression: they speak loftily.*

*They set their mouths against the heavens,
and their tongue walketh through the earth.*

*Therefore his people return hither: and
waters of a full cup are wrung out of them.*

*And they say, How doth God know?
And is there knowledge in the most high?*

*Behold these are the ungodly who
prosper in the world: they increase in riches."*

– Psalms 73:1-12.

David could not understand how people through unrighteous means could amass so much wealth and yet still appear as if all is well with them. David could not understand how people could gather wealth through cheating, deceit, violence, oppression, corruption and wickedness and yet appear as if they are at peace.

David was so curious to know and the reason for his curiosity was that he was already falling into the temptation of pursuing wealth via wrong means as he saw fit with the corrupt and wicked men of his days. Men who tend to benefit and profit from the misery of others. But thank God David got the answer he was looking for.

Hear him:

*"When I thought to know this,
it was too painful for me;*

*Until I went into the sanctuary of God;
then understood I their end;*

*Surely thou didst set them in slippery places:
thou castedst them down unto destruction.*

How are they brought into desolation, as in a moment. They are utterly consumed with terrors.

*As a dream when one awaketh;
so, O Lord, when thou awakest,
thou shalt despise their image.*

*Thus my heart was grieved,
and I was pricked in my reins.*

*So foolish was I, and ignorant;
I was as a beast before thee."*

– Psalms 73:16-22.

David was so ignorant and foolish about ungodly men. Only a fool will envy the riches of the wicked. Only ignorance will envy wealth gotten by wrong means. When understanding caught up with David, David knew better. Every wealth gotten by wrong means will surely end with wrong things. Every wealth gotten through wrong means cannot escape wrong things.

Wrong means will always generate wrong things. Wrong means and wrong things always go together; they can't separate. Watch it! If your means to wealth is not good, then your wealth is not sure. Righteousness is the greatest assurance any man can have. Nothing places a guarantee over your life like righteousness.

Israel was in slavery for over four hundred years. Their situation was so pathetic. Their suffering was unbearable. In their misery, they cried out to God for help and deliverance. And in responding to them God sent Moses to deliver them out of the hand of Pharaoh into the land of Canaan–a land full of milk and honey.

"And the LORD said,
I have surely seen the affliction of my people
which are in Egypt, and have heard
their cry by reason of their taskmasters;
for I know their sorrows;

And I am come down to deliver them
out of the hand of the Egyptians,
and to bring them up out of that land
unto a good land and a large,
unto a land flowing with milk and honey;
unto the place of the Canaanites;
and the Hittites; and the Amorites;
and the Perizzites, and the Hivites, and the Jebusites.

Now therefore, behold,
the cry of the children of Israel is come

*unto me; and I have also seen the oppression
wherewith the Egyptians oppress them.*

*Come now therefore,
and I will send thee unto Pharaoh;
that thou mayest bring forth my people the
children of Israel out of Egypt. "*

– Exodus 3:7-10.

This was God's plan for the children of Israel-to bring them out of bondage and slavery from Egypt into liberty and destiny to the land of Canaan and Moses was called upon by God to carry out this great plan. But before God actually released Moses to go to Egypt for the deliverance of Israel, God had to empower the rod of Moses for signs and wonders before Pharaoh in Egypt.

*"And thou shalt take this rod in
thine hand, wherewith thou shalt do signs."*

– Exodus 4:17.

Every sign and wonder Moses did in Egypt, Moses did through his rod. As such the rod of Moses was a channel of divine proofs. The rod of Moses was a means for the release of the supernatural. As Moses approached Pharaoh in Egypt for the deliverance of the children of Israel, Pharaoh King of Egypt demanded for a miracle. Pharaoh demanded for a sign.

In response to Pharaoh, Moses threw down his rod and it became a serpent. Just as Moses had his own rod for signs and wonders, the magicians in Pharaoh's court also had their own rods for their own signs and wonders. And so, as Moses threw down his rod and it became a serpent, the magicians also threw down their own rods and they also became serpents.

*"And Moses and Aaron went in unto Pharaoh,
and they did so as the LORD had commanded:
and Aaron cast down his rod before Pharaoh,
and before his servants and it became a serpent.*

> *Then Pharaoh also called the wise men*
> *and the sorcerers: now the magicians of Egypt,*
> *they also did in like manner with their enchantments.*
>
> *For they cast down every man his rod,*
> *and they became serpents: but Aaron's rod*
> *swallowed up their rods."*
>
> *– Exodus 7:10-12.*

It was a dramatic show of serpents before Pharaoh, king of Egypt. While Moses' rod became just one serpent, the rods of the Egyptians became many serpents. And so, it was serpents against serpent as it was rods against rod. At the end, the serpent of Moses swallowed up the serpents of the Egyptians. The rod of Moses swallowed the rods of the Egyptians.

Both parties (Moses and the Egyptians) all ended up with serpents from their rods. All the serpents came through certain means. The serpents either came through the rod of Moses or through the rods of the Egyptians. After Moses laid down his rod and it became a serpent, Pharaoh in following suit commanded not just anybody but certain people to throw down their rods.

MANY AGAINST ONE

These people were the ones to stand up against Moses. These selected ones were the ones to compete against the rod of Moses and the selected people called upon by Pharaoh were the wise men; the magicians and the sorcerers. These were the men whose means brought about the serpents that ended up in the belly of Moses' serpent.

The rod of Moses and the rods of Pharaoh through the wise men; the magicians and the sorcerers, reveal the various means through which men arrive at their various results and the end of those results.

While some pursue righteous means to wealth, others in the guise or company of the wise men seek wealth through cunning, deception and manipulation. Wise men in this regard refer to those who specialize in using their senses to cheat and deprive others. They engage in manipulation, lying and all manner of dirty schemes to gain wealth.

THE DECEIVER WILL BE DECEIVED

Like the serpent in the Garden of Eden, they engage in twisting and ignoring the truth. Any wealth gotten through lying, cheating, deception and manipulation; has no future. You can't cheat, deceive and manipulate people and expect to escape the corollary. There will always be dire consequences to face.

The sorcerers and magicians were another group Pharaoh called. These ones refer to people who use satanic and occult means to access results. Any occult means to wealth will undoubtedly fail. Your only sure means to wealth is righteousness. For wealth to flow into your life, righteousness must become your lifestyle.

(2) DIVINE REVELATIONS

Another force that positions you for the transfer of wealth is divine revelation. Wealth flows in the direction of divine revelations. Wealth moves in the direction of divine revelations. The unimaginable wealth that was transferred to Egypt was as a result of the divine revelations Pharaoh had.

But the big question is how can you access divine revelations? How can you tap into the covenant flow of divine revelations?

*"Howbeit we speak wisdom among them
that are perfect; yet not the wisdom
of this world, nor of the princes of this world,
that come to nought.*

*But we speak the wisdom of God
in a mystery, even the hidden wisdom,
which God ordained before the world unto our glory:*

*Which none of the princes of this world knew;
for had they known it, they would not have
crucified the Lord of glory.*

> *But as it is written, Eye hath not seen,*
> *nor ear heard, neither have entered into*
> *the heart of man, the things which God hath*
> *prepared for them that love him.*
>
> *But God hath revealed them unto his Spirit:*
> *for the Spirit searcheth all things, yea,*
> *the deep things of God.*
>
> *For what man knoweth the things of a man,*
> *save the spirit of man which is in him?*
> *Even so the things of God knoweth no man,*
> *but the Spirit of God"*
>
> *– I Corinthians 2:6-11.*

The Holy Spirit who is the Spirit of God is in charge of divine revelations. Every divine revelation is by the Spirit of God. Every divine revelation is a function of the Spirit of God. The Holy Spirit is your access to divine revelations. The Holy Spirit is your connection to divine revelations. You can't access divine revelations on your own. You can't access divine revelations by your strength.

You need the Holy Spirit to tap into divine revelations. Until you connect with the Holy Spirit, you cannot connect with divine revelations. Divine revelations are totally impossible without the Holy Spirit. The Holy Spirit is your principal source to divine revelations. Every divine revelation flows through the Holy Spirit.

> *"Howbeit when he, the Spirit of truth is come,*
> *he will guide you into all truth: for he shall*
> *not speak of himself; but whatsoever*
> *he shall hear, that shall he speak:*
> *and he will show you things to come."*
>
> *– John 16:13*

The business of the Holy Spirit with you is to show you things. The principal job of the Holy Spirit among other things is to reveal things to you. The Holy Spirit helps you to see things. The Holy Spirit helps to open your eyes to things. Things become open and clear with the help of the Holy Spirit. Certain things don't just reveal themselves. Certain things don't just show themselves.

We live in a world where most things are essentially hidden. We live in a world where so many things are covered. The Holy Spirit brings hidden things to light. The Holy Spirit uncovers things that are covered. The Holy Spirit sheds light on darkness. Nothing can be hidden with the Holy Spirit. Everything is open with the Holy Spirit. This is why you need the Holy Spirit.

CONNECT WITH REVELATIONS

You need to make a connection with the Holy Spirit. Every attempt to access divine revelations without the Holy Spirit is an attempt in futility. Every attempt to tap into divine revelations without the Holy Spirit will only end in frustration.

When Jesus died on the cross, the veil in the temple was torn from top to bottom. Before the veil was torn, nobody knew what was behind the veil. No one except the high priest had access to that part of the temple. But immediately the veil was torn from top to bottom, everything behind the veil was revealed. Everything behind the veil was no longer hidden.

Everything was open. Anyone who wanted to see could now see what was hidden behind the veil. With the torn veil, seeing was no more selective rather seeing became a choice. If you want to see, you will see.

> *"And Jesus cried with a loud voice,*
> *and gave up the ghost.*
> *And the veil of the temple was rent in twain*
> *from the top to the bottom."*
>
> *– Mark 15:37-38.*

Just as the veil was torn from top to bottom as a result of the death of Jesus Christ on the cross with everything that was hidden behind the veil now revealed and opened for everyone to see, in like manner, the Holy Spirit helps us to see things that are veiled. The Holy Spirit exposes things to us by removing the veils that are before our eyes.

Life is essentially hidden. Life is covered. The world and the things that constitute the beauties and treasures of this world are mostly covered in veils. There are veils preventing men from accessing what they should access. There are veils stopping men from connecting with things they should connect with. There are veils limiting and confining people. These veils are real and they are all around us.

> *"And not as Moses, which put a vail over his face that the children of Israel could not steadfastly look to the end of that which is abolished:*
>
> *But their minds were blinded: for until this day remaineth the same vail untaken away in the reading of the old testament: which veil is done away in Christ.*
>
> *But even unto this day, when Moses is read, the vail is upon their heart. Nevertheless when it shall turn to the Lord, the vail shall be taken away."*
>
> *– II Corinthians 3:13-16.*

> *"And in this mountain shall the Lord of hosts make unto all people a feast of fat things, a feast of wines on the lees, of fat things full of marrow, of wines on the lees well refined.*
>
> *And he will destroy on this mountain the face of the covering cast over all nations."*

– Isaiah 25:6-7.

There is an urgent need for the veils around you to be removed. Until veils are removed, things will not be revealed. For things to be revealed, veils must be removed. There has to be an uncovering if there is to be an opening. Every divine revelation is a product of the removal of veils.

> *"And if any man think that he knoweth any thing, he knoweth nothing, yet as he ought to know."*
>
> *– I Corinthians 8:2.*

No man can know everything. No man, no matter his level in life, can outgrow revelations. As long as there are things to know, there will always be veils to be removed. As long as there are things to be revealed, there will be veils to be removed. Divine revelation is all about the Holy Spirit removing the veils before you and exposing things to you from time to time.

When Saul met with Jesus on his way to Damascus, Saul's encounter with Jesus resulted in a turning point in his life. And the turning point of Saul's life was the falling off of scales from his eyes.

> *"And Ananias went his way, and entered into the house, and putting his hands upon him said, Brother Saul, the LORD, even Jesus, that appeared unto thee on the way as thou camest hath sent me, that thou mightest receive thy sight, and be filled with the Holy Ghost.*
>
> *And immediately there fell from his eyes as it had been scales: and he received sight forthwith, and arose, and was baptized.*
>
> *And when he had received meat, he was strengthened. Then was Saul certain days with the disciples which were at Damascus.*

> *And straightway he preached Christ in
> the synagogues, that he is the Son of God."*

– Acts 9:17-20.

Immediately the scales fell off from Saul's eyes, Saul's mission changed. Saul whose sole mission was to capture and imprison every Christian within his reach was now preaching the gospel. All this while, before Saul met with Jesus, Saul had scales (which are also a type of veil) over his eyes which were not obvious until his encounter with Jesus. Before the scales fell off from Saul's eyes, Saul was busy persecuting and destroying the church and Christians.

> *"As for Saul, he made havoc of the church,
> entering into every house, and hailing men
> and women, committed them to prison.*
>
> *Therefore they that were scattered
> abroad went every where preaching the word."*

– Acts 8:3-4.

Christians scattered and traveled very far just to escape the evil reach of Saul. Saul was a terror to the church. Saul was a living nightmare to the Christians. And yet Saul felt that persecuting and destroying the church was the right thing to do. Instead of preaching the gospel, Saul was destroying the gospel.

Saul was doing the exact opposite of what he was supposed to be doing. Saul was doing what was wrong thinking he was doing what was right. Saul was doing what he was not supposed to be doing and yet he did not know, all because of the scales over his eyes. Saul was far from his destiny all because of the scales over his eyes.

WHEN YOUR EYES ARE OPENED

Saul was in direct opposition to his destiny and he did not even know it all because of the scales over his eyes. But when the scales fell off from his eyes, Saul changed. A lot of people are doing what they are not supposed to be doing all because of the scales over their eyes.

A lot of people have not even started doing what they should be doing. A lot of people are destroying what they should be protecting. Like Saul, a lot of people are doing the wrong things thinking they are doing the right thing. A lot of people are in direct opposition to their destinies.

So many don't know it and its all because of the scales over their eyes. A lot of people are standing against their own success. A lot of people are standing against their own wealth and happiness.

AN EXPERIENCE TO BE DESIRED
A lot of people are standing against their own destiny. A lot of people are far from their destiny thinking they are close to their destiny and yet just like Saul, they don't know it. And the reason why they don't know it is because of the scales over their eyes. So many like Saul are destroying their destinies thinking they are fulfilling their destinies. They are yet to see what is behind the veil.

They think they know but they don't know. They think they are working but they are wasting. They think they are seeing but they are sinking. They are yet to experience the falling off of the scales from their eyes. And because veils are not things that are obvious, they assume that all is well and good even with the irregularities that seem to abound.

This is why the veils must be removed. The scales must fall off. Until you see what is behind the veil your life will be in vain. Until you see what is behind, you cannot get ahead. You need to see what is hidden about you. You need to know what you don't know about your life and the things that concern you.

You need insights into the dark areas of your life. This is why you need revelations. Divine revelations are too important. Divine revelations take you beyond the veil. Divine revelations takes off the scales from your eyes. Divine revelations gives you access to the truth. Divine revelations connects you to destiny. Divine revelations makes you do what you should be doing whether it makes sense to people or not.

When Saul who was destroying the gospel, started preaching the gospel, people were amazed. They were shocked. They were surprised. It was too unbelievable.

> *"And straightway he preached Christ*
> *in the synagogue, that he is the Son of God.*
>
> *But all that heard him were amazed,*
> *and said, is not this he that destroyed them*
> *which called on his name in Jerusalem,*
> *and came hither for that intent, that he might*
> *bring them bound unto the chief priests?*
>
> *But Saul increased the more in strength and*
> *confounded the Jews which dwelt at Damascus,*
> *proving that this is very Christ."*
>
> *— Acts 9:20-22.*

Saul who was disputing Christ before, was now proving that Christ is the savior. All the shocks were all as a result of the scales that fell off from Saul's eyes. All the surprises were all as a result of the veils that were removed from Saul's eyes. All the wonders were all as a result of the revelations that caught up with Saul.

Your access to wealth may be as a result of something unbelievable. Your access to wealth may be as a result of something that will shock and surprise everyone around you including yourself. Your access to wealth maybe as a result of something you may never have done or thought of doing before. Your access to wealth maybe in direct opposition to your education, certifications, status and even belief.

Saul was passionate about persecuting the Christians. He even went to the extent of obtaining authority to wreck havoc to the Christians. This was what placed him on his way to Damascus.

> *"And Saul yet breathing out threatenings and slaughter against the disciples of the Lord, went unto the high priest.*
>
> *And desired of him letters to Damascus to the synagogue, that if he found any of this way, whether they were men or women, he might bring them bound unto Jerusalem."*
>
> *– Acts 9:1-2.*

Destroying the church was Saul's desire but yet it was not his destiny. Persecuting the Christians was Saul's passion but it was not his portion. Your access to wealth maybe something not within the scope of your supposed passion and desire.

Your access to wealth maybe something that is not popular with you or people; something that people may not support-not because it is bad or wrong in itself but because it does not make sense to people or it's not appealing to people.

CHECK YOUR PASSION

Just like Saul, so many are fired up by the wrong passions and desires. They are passionate but their passions are wrong; they are passionate about the wrong things. They are driven but their drive is wrong. Their drive is off track. Their drive is off key. They are driven by the wrong things. They may not know it but it is the way it is.

Many are engineered by the wrong passion. They are not supposed to be passionate about what they are passionate about. Their passion is wrong. Your passion can be off course. Your passion can be wrong, not because it is bad or wrong on its own but because it is wrong for you. It might be right for someone else but can be wrong for you.

What is right for you might be wrong for others because it just does not serve or it is not supposed to be. And what is right for others might be wrong for you. This is the dicey path of life. As such, passion is not enough to succeed. Passion is not a sure pointer to success or wealth.

You must check your passion. You must check your drive. What is driving you in life? What is pushing you in life? The fact that you are driven, does not mean you are winning. What matters is not the fact that you are driven. No! Far from it. What really matters is what is driving you. If your drive is wrong, your life is doomed.

THE ONLY WAY

Passion can be wrong. Passion can mislead. Passion can deceive. But how can you know if you are being driven by the right passion or not? How can you know if you are being fired in the right direction or not? You might think you are right; the people around you might think or say you are on track; you may have the support and the goodwill of so many but just like Saul, you maybe off track.

You maybe off course. You maybe wrong. The support of people in itself is not enough to give to you the credibility you need to move in the right direction. The support of people does not make you right. The goodwill of many does not mean you are heading in the right direction. You can be supported to hell. You can be supported to destruction.

BE WISE

You can be supported to doom. And one thing about the support of people is that it can shift. Support can shift. Support can change. Those whom you think are supporting you can plot against you. Those whom you think are your pillars can become your killers.

Pillars can become killers. Supporters can become opposers. Goodwill can grow wings. The goodwill of people can change with the blink of an eye and yet without a cause or reason. So many things defy reason. The support of people is like the weather.

The goodwill of people is like the weather. It can change at any moment even without a sign. And so, while you have the goodwill of people, enjoy it but don't bank on it. It will not be wise if you do so. It is not wise to bank on the support of people. It is not wise to throw your whole weight on people.

People can change at any moment and when they can change, they change in ways that can be so shocking and embarrassing. People are creatures of surprise. If you follow the support of people, you will lose your way. If bank on people, you will regret it. Support is not enough.

THERE IS SOMETHING SUPERIOR

The support of people is not enough to tell that you on the right track. The endorsement of people is not enough to show that you are moving in the right direction. Intelligence also is not enough to show that you are on or off track. Intelligence is limited in its own way.

There are so many things that defy intelligence. Intelligence is not the ultimate. Intelligence is not revelation and revelation is not by intelligence. Intelligence is the effort of man while revelation is the effort of the Spirit. And of course, the best of men is inferior to the least of the Spirit.

Revelation is superior to intelligence. Deep things are most times not given to the wise. Experience cannot also tell if you are on track or not Experience has its limits. The only thing that can tell if you on track or off track is revelation.

Without revelation, you are lost and gone. This is why after so many years of labours and sweat, so many still end up with regrets. All of a sudden, they just found out that they were working for nothing. All of a sudden, nothing makes sense anymore, even their lives no more makes sense. All of a sudden, their life is beclouded with so much regrets. If only they had known. Life is a mystery. Wealth is a mystery.

When Saul began to preach, the Jews plotted against him.

*"And after that many days were fulfilled,
the Jews took counsel to kill him.*

*But their laying await was known to Saul. v5,j
And they watched the gates day and night to kill him.*

Then the disciples took him by night and let

him down by the wall in a basket. "

- Acts 9:23-25.

Saul was now a target.

Your access to wealth and destiny may demand great risks. Your path to wealth might gather so much oppositions that you might tempted to lose direction. Wealth is like a puzzle. Your wealth may not come to you the way you think it will come to you. This is why you must not confine yourself to yourself.

You must not confine yourself to your sense, knowledge or experience alone. You must not confine yourself to only your thoughts and decisions.

BEYOND BOUNDARIES AND FORMULARS

You must not restrict yourself to the prevailing norms, traditions and boundaries that has held many captive. Tradition is one of the greatest enemies of wealth. Boundaries is one of the greatest obstacles to wealth. Wealth is innovative. Wealth is creative. Wealth will take you beyond boundaries. Wealth will extend you.

Wealth is not necessarily a product of what has been rather wealth is a product of what can be. Wealth is the future. Wealth is capturing the future. Wealth is capturing the essence. Wealth lies in seeing beyond now. Wealth goes beyond today. Wealth lies in seeing tomorrow.

WEALTH IS INNOVATIVE

Wealth lies in seizing tomorrow. Wealth lies in taking the initiative. The way it was done yesterday is not necessarily the way it will be done today. This is why, as you make your journey to wealth, you must be very careful of formulas. Wealth is not just a formula. Wealth is not in formulas. Wealth is an invention.

Wealth is in innovations. If you must access wealth, you must not confine yourself to formulas. If you must access wealth, you must not confine yourself to just your secular education, certificates, experience or skills.

Don't confine yourself to anything because anything can bring you everything.

Anything can bring you wealth. This is why divine revelation is needed. Divine revelations go beyond your thoughts to connect you with the source.

HOW YOU CAN ACCESS REVELATIONS THROUGH THE HOLY SPIRIT

It was prayer that caused the scales from Saul's eyes to fall off thereby opening Saul up to the divine revelations that he needed.

> *"And Ananias went his way, and entered into the house; and putting his hands on him said, Brother Saul, the Lord, even Jesus, that appeared unto thee in the way as thou camest, hath sent me, that mightest receive thy sight, and be filled with the Holy Ghost.*
>
> *And immediately there fell from his eyes as it had been scales; and he received sight forthwith, and arose, and was baptized."*
>
> *– Acts 9:17-18.*

Prayer is your access to divine revelations. Prayer is your key to divine revelations. Prayer is your gateway to divine revelations. Divine revelations require prayers. Divine revelations don't just come for the sake of coming. Divine revelations answer to prayers. When you pray, the Holy Spirit is moved to release divine revelations.

When you pray, the Holy Spirit goes into action to give you access to divine revelations. And so what prayers does in regard to divine revelations is that prayers put the Holy Spirit to work on your behalf. Prayers prompts the Holy Spirit. Prayers motions the Holy Spirit.

THE GATEWAY

Even though prayer is your access to divine revelations, the Holy Spirit is the principal source of divine revelations. What prayer does is to connect you to the Holy Spirit. This is why the Holy Spirit responds to your prayers and in turn connects you to divine revelations.

Even though the Holy Spirit is in charge of divine revelations, the Holy Spirit will not just dish out divine revelations to you without your prayers. Your prayer is the power that moves the Holy Spirit in line with your desired divine revelations. In your quest for divine revelations, prayer is very essential.

"Call unto me, and I will answer thee, and show you great and mighty things which thou knowest not."

– Jeremiah 33:3.

Before there can be a *'showing,'* there has to a *'calling.'* Nothing can be shown to you unless you call out to God. Your 'calling' is what positions you for your *'showing.'* *'Showing'* answers to *'calling.'* Your prayer is a spiritual indication to the Holy Spirit that you need a divine revelation.

JOURNEY TO WEALTH

WEALTH IS FUNDAMENTALLY A PERSONAL CHOICE

BY: JOSHUA GREAT

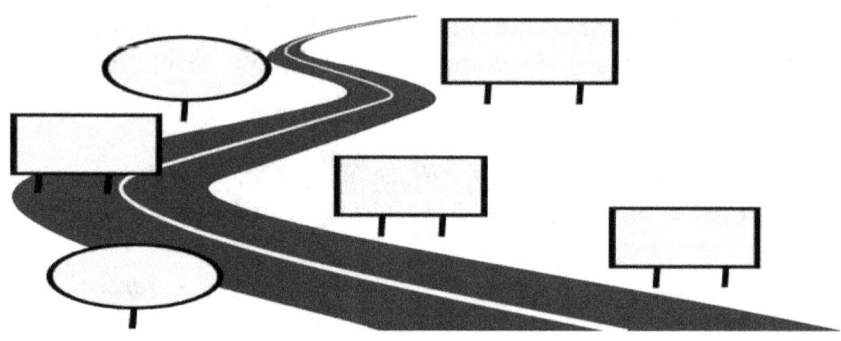

CHAPTER SIX
YOUR WELLS

Without any doubt, Egypt became unimaginably wealthy because of the famine. Egypt was able to access unusual dimensions of wealth because of the famine. But by and large, Egypt's vast and immense wealth came as a result of the divine revelations Pharaoh had. The divine revelation Pharaoh had was what delivered the treasures of the world to Egypt.

> *"And it came to pass at the end of two full years, that Pharaoh dreamed: and, behold, he stood by the river.*
>
> *And behold, there came out of the river seven well favoured kine and fatfleshed; and they fed in a meadow.*
>
> *And behold, seven other kine came up after them out of the river, ill favoured and leanfleshed; and stood by the other kine upon the brink of the river.*
>
> *And the ill favoured and leanfleshed kine did eat up the seven well favoured and fat kine. So Pharaoh awoke.*
>
> *And he slept and dreamed the second time: and, behold, seven ears of corn came up upon one stalk, rank and good.*
>
> *And, behold, seven thin ears blasted with the east wind sprung up after them.*
>
> *And the seven thin ears devoured the seven rank and full ears. And Pharaoh awoke, and behold, it was a dream."*

– Genesis 41:1-7.

This was Pharaoh's dream. But a long time ago, long before Pharaoh had his dreams, Joseph already had his own dreams; dreams that shed light not only on the destiny of Joseph but also on the destiny of nations; dreams that will later connect with the dreams of Pharaoh.

Joseph's dreams:

"And Joseph dreamed a dream; and he told it his brethren; and they hated him yet the more.

And he said unto them, Hear, I pray you, this dream which I dreamed.

For, behold, we were binding sheaves in the field, and lo, my sheaf arose, and also stood upright, and, behold, your sheaves stood round about, and made obeisance to my sheaf.

And his brethren said to him, Shalt thou indeed reign over us? Or Shalt thou indeed have dominion over us? And they hated him yet the more for his dreams, and for his words.

And he dreamed yet another dream, and told it his brethren, and, said, behold, I have dreamed a dream more, and behold the sun and the moon and the eleven stars made obeisance to me."

– Genesis 37:5-9.

These dreams were not just empty pictures of a deep sleep. They were the divine revelations of Joseph's destiny. What was hidden concerning Joseph's destiny was gradually brought to the open. Joseph had a great destiny. Joseph had a destiny that even his own family could not accept or understand. But by and large that was Joseph's destiny and there was nothing anybody could do about it.

From the grand scheme of things, there was a powerful connection between the dreams of Joseph and the dreams of Pharaoh. Joseph had two dreams; Pharaoh also had two dreams. The two dreams of Joseph was one split into two and the same also goes for Pharaoh's dreams.

THE JOURNEY OF DESTINY

Pharaoh's dreams were actually meant to usher in the reality of Joseph's destiny. Pharaoh's dreams were meant to bring to pass the manifestation of Joseph's dreams. Joseph's dreams were the revelation of his destiny but Pharaoh's dreams were for the fulfilment of Joseph's destiny.

The reality of Joseph's destiny was actually in the revelation of Pharaoh's dreams. The time line between when Joseph had his dreams and when Pharaoh had his own dreams was a very long one. The time gap between Joseph's dreams and Pharaoh's dreams was no small time. But despite the huge time gap, despite the very long-time line, the dreams of Joseph and Pharaoh were deeply connected by destiny.

DESTINY IS A MYSTERY

Look at the incidents and the points of connection as regards Joseph and Pharaoh as their lines crossed even with the different time phases that stretched over their lives and destinies.

Immediately Joseph had his dreams and declared them to his family, all hell broke loose. Joseph's entire brothers hated him. Already there was a hate agenda against Joseph from his brothers because of Jacob's love for Joseph over his brothers.

Of all the children Jacob had, Joseph was the one Jacob loved the most and Jacob didn't even bother to hide it. He openly declared that Joseph was his favourite child. And Joseph suffered for it.

"Now Israel loved Joseph more than
all his children, because he was the son of
his old age: and he made him a coat of many colors.

And when his brethren saw that their
father loved him more than all his brethren,
they hated him, and could not speak peaceably unto him."

– Genesis 37:3-4.

When favoritism enters into a family setting, it disrupts and destroys the family. It paves the way for jealousy and hatred to come in. A situation where siblings become rivals is not healthy at all; a situation where the family line becomes a battle front is totally unsuitable. This is what happens when a parent shows or makes one child better than the rest.

When a child is show cased as the best above the rest, rest ceases for that child and for that family. When a child is approved over the rest, a big problem is being prepped to explode. When a child becomes beloved above the rest, that child becomes destroyed amongst the rest.

When a parent begins to love one child over the others, that child becomes endangered; you place that child at a big risk and a great disadvantage. Loving one child more than the other children is bad and dangerous for a child. Instead of helping, it will kill the child. It will automatically make the other children hate the so called favored child.

DON'T MAKE YOU CHILD A TARGET
Most times hatred among children has always been a result of parents loving one child above the rest. A situation where children have to compete for the love and attention of their parents as against another child who has it lavished on him or her just like that, is practically upsetting, unhealthy and dangerous.

As a parent, don't favor one child over the others. Don't patronize loving one child no matter the reason above the others. If you actually love that child above your other children then don't show it. You have a duty not to show it. Once you show it, it becomes show time.

WHAT YOU DO FOR ONE DO FOR ALL

Favored children are always targeted children. Don't destroy your children. Whatever you buy for one, endeavor to buy for all. Whatever you do for one, endeavor to do for all. Maintain the balance amongst your children by appreciating and correcting them individually and collectively.

The feeling must be mutual and not special. It must be inclusive and not exclusive. Be a loving parent to all your children. Your children deserve your unconditional love and attention whether they are good or bad; you owe them that. Joseph had to endure the hatred of all his brothers because of his father's particular love for him.

There was already a hate agenda against Joseph from his brothers. But when Joseph declared his dreams, the level of hatred against Joseph from his brother's sky-rocketed so much so that Joseph's brothers wanted to get rid of him by all means. Eventually, as a means to an end, Joseph was sold as a slave by his brothers to traveling merchant men.

"Come, and let us sell him to the Ishmeelites,
and let not our hands be upon him,
for he is our brother and our flesh.
And his brethren were content.

Then there passed by Midianites merchantmen;
and they drew and lifted up Joseph out of the pit,
and sold Joseph to the Ishmeelites for twenty
pieces of silver, and they brought Joseph into Egypt."

– Genesis 37:27-28.

By selling Joseph off to total strangers, Joseph's brothers, in their bitter hatred, wanted to end Joseph's dreams and by extension his destiny. But instead of ending Joseph's dreams, they only helped in kick starting his dreams. By selling Joseph off to strangers, Joseph was brought to Egypt, his place of destiny.

The hatred of Joseph's brothers brought Joseph to his place of destiny. No true destiny can ever escape the bite of opposition. No true destiny can ever escape the reality of enemies. As long as you have a destiny, you will surely have enemies.

Where there is a destiny, there will surely be enemies. But no matter the enemies after your destiny, they can't stop your destiny. No opposition can stop your destiny. No amount or level of hatred from anybody can stop your destiny. The oppositions of people cannot stop your destiny.

FRUITS ATTRACT STONES

Destiny is not a walk in the park. The road to destiny is full of so many oppositions and so many enemies. People will try to stop you by all means possible from becoming what you are destined to become. People will attempt to fight you in any and every way they can all because of your destiny. But you need to know that nobody can stop your destiny.

Your destiny is unstoppable. No attack can truncate the reality of your great destiny. People don't throw stones at a tree that has no friuts. People will only throw stones at a tree that has fruits. No one has any business with a tree that has no fruits. A tree that has no fruits, has no attraction.

A tree that has no fruits will always be at rest. But a tree that has fruits will never be at rest. There is no rest with destiny. Every rest with destiny will only rob you of your best with destiny. Destiny forbids rest. Destiny naturally attracts attacks. Attacks will always come after destiny.

OPPOSITION IS A DRIVER

People will never mind a tree that has no fruits. People will only mind trees that have fruits. If people are minding you, it is because you carry something-you carry destiny. Oppositions will always dot the path of destiny. As long as you carry destiny, stones will come at you. But no matter the stones that come at you, they cannot bring you down. No matter how hard the wind blows, the mountain cannot bow to it.

Just like the hatred of Joseph's brothers, where instead of destroying Joseph, it served only to help Joseph, in like manner, every hatred and opposition you encounter in your pursuit to destiny, only drives your destiny to fulfilment. Every opposition against your destiny, only positions your destiny for good.

Every stone hauled at your destiny, only strengthens your destiny. Opposition is the major drive of destiny. Opposition is the core strength of destiny. Without oppositions, people will grow lazy with destiny. Destiny moves towards fulfilment with oppositions. Every destruction aimed at your destiny only restructures your destiny.

Satan felt that by killing Jesus, it would all be over. What Satan did not know was that by crucifying Jesus, he was actually helping in the fulfilment of the destiny of Jesus.

> *"Which none of the princes of this world knew: for had they known it, they would not have crucified the Lord of glory."*
>
> *– I Corinthians 2:8.*

All Satan would have done to stop Jesus was to do nothing. Do nothing; say nothing. In fact, Satan would have sought to protect and keep Jesus from dying. Just by protecting Jesus and doing nothing to attack Jesus, Satan would have defeated Jesus. Just by doing nothing, Satan would have brought Jesus to nothing despite all his miracles.

Sometimes, doing nothing does plenty. Sometimes, doing nothing serves more than doing something. Sometimes, saying nothing serves more than saying something. Sometimes, being passive is far more effective than being active. There are times when the best way to deal with your enemies is to say nothing and do nothing.

A SPECIAL TIME

There are times when the best way to handle or resolve a situation is to do nothing and say nothing. There are times when nothing does plenty and there are times when plenty does nothing. And sometimes, doing nothing can prove to be so difficult. But whether difficult or not, you must know when these times dawns on you and respond accordingly.

Just as Satan, in order to destroy Jesus would have sought to protect instead of attacking Jesus, in like manner, there are times when the best way to silence your enemies is to protect your enemies. Sometimes, protection can serve the purpose of destruction.

Sometimes, peace can serve the purpose of war; love can serve the purpose of hate; gathering can serve the purpose of scattering; living can serve the purpose of dying; rising can serve the purpose of falling; success can serve the purpose of failure; light can serve the purpose of darkness and something can serve the purpose of nothing. Most things aren't really as they are.

There is a twist to everything in life. Life itself is a twist. Life is not a straight road. Life is not straight at all. No one has ever gone through life the way he or she planned. Life has a way of altering your plans, no matter how well conceived or well-intentioned your plans may be. This is why life is full of so many bends.

BENDING BUT NOT BLENDING
Anyone who must rise or succeed in this life must definitely know how to bend with the many bends of life. You must know how to bend with life if you must go far or amount to anything meaningful in this life. If you don't know how to bend, you will end.

So many in their ignorance and innocence don't understand the bending nature of life. Many don't know how to bend. Many think or feel that to bend means to compromise. Many think that to bend means to be crooked or to bend means to blend. Many don't know the difference between bending and blending.

Many don't know how to bend without blending. And because many really don't know how to bend with life, so many are confused, disappointed, bitter and frustrated with life. So many wonder why life is the way it is to them? So many wonder, why life is so cruel and unfair to them despite all they have done? Many even go to the extreme of wondering why they are so unlucky in life?

It's so pathetic and painful to bear these thoughts but that is the sour reality of so many. There is a mysterious underlaying paradox that is webbed into the fabrics of our everyday reality and existence.

Understanding this mysterious paradox, is very crucial because it is what gives you an edge in this life. This mystery is what keeps your head above the overwhelming waters of life that seeks to drown you just as it has drowned so many.

SILENCE OPPOSITIONS

The scripture says, if your enemy is hungry, give him food. If your enemy is thirsty, give him water, by doing so, you are heaping coals of fire on the head of your enemies. Your good is not doing your enemies any good or any favor. If for anything, your good kills your enemies. Your good eats up your enemies.

It is not every good that serves the purpose of good and it is not every evil that serves the purpose of evil. This is the strange twist of life. Sometimes, good serves the purpose of evil. Good can serve the purpose of silencing oppositions and dealing with enemies. Sometimes, the weapon you need to destroy your enemies is good.

Just as every sword has two sides, good can be good and good can also be bad. Good can serve the purpose of good and can also serve the purpose of bad. In like manner, bad can be bad and bad can also be good. Evil can serve a good purpose. Evil can turn out good and good can turn out evil.

UNDERSTANDING THE TWIST

All Satan was to do to stop Jesus would have been nothing. Satan would have just ignored Jesus. Satan would have just allowed Jesus to grow old. In growing old, the plan of redemption would have been aborted. But he failed with Jesus. If Satan failed before, he will fail again. If Satan failed with Jesus, he will fail with you because he cannot stay doing nothing.

Satan cannot stay without doing something. The same old pattern keeps playing out. And this is one of the weakness of the devil. Without enemies, there will be no destiny. You need enemies to fulfill your destiny. Enemies are the forces of destiny. Enemies are the platforms on which destiny stands.

ENEMIES ARE REAL

Enemies are the ones that push destiny into reality. There is no destiny that has ever been fulfilling without the major contributions of enemies. Enemies give birth to destiny. Enemies mould destiny. While you may not like the idea of enemies, the reality of enemies is always for the good of your destiny.

Thank God for your enemies, for without them, your destiny will never become a reality. Every problem that they give to you in pursuit of your destiny is actually for the good of your destiny. Every hardship you encounter today is actually for the good of your destiny tomorrow.

> *"And we know that all things work together for good to them that love God, to them who are the called according to his purpose."*
>
> *– Romans 8:28.*

Enemies drive destiny into action. Or else how would Joseph have gotten to Egypt-his place of destiny-if not by the deliberate hatred of his brothers? Jacob's love for Joseph was so obvious that it would not have allowed Joseph to separate from his father in the pursuit of his destiny. And there is no way Joseph would have fulfilled his destiny in Canaan land or anywhere else apart from Egypt.

Enemies in the name of brothers and family drove Joseph to destiny. Enemies can come in any shape. They can come in any form. They can come as parents. They can come as siblings. They can come as uncles and aunties. They can come as friends and colleagues.

Enemies can come as neighbours. This is why you must be very vigilant especially to those who enjoy the awesome benefit of your trust and confidence. Life requires vigilance. Life calls for vigilance. In whichever form your enemies may choose to present themselves to you, you must not be mistaken or sentimental.

Upon arrival in Egypt, Joseph was further sold to Potiphar- a man with access to Pharaoh - the king of Egypt.

> *"And the Midianites sold him into Egypt unto Potiphar, an officer of Pharaoh's and captain of the guard."*
>
> *– Genesis 37:36.*

Joseph was getting close to destiny but not in the way he thought he would. Every situation; every incident, was actually connecting the dots in favor of Joseph's destiny even though he did not know it. Joseph, now a slave of Potiphar, had no choice but to work hard and slave for Potiphar.

What kind of future does a slave have? Does a slave really have a future? Oh Yes! A slave with a destiny does have a future and not just a future but a great one at that. It does not matter what condition or situation you may be, when destiny comes calling, things will fall into place for you.

While in Potiphar's house, God blessed Potiphar because of Joseph. But along the line, something happened and Joseph was thrown into prison. Joseph was falsely accused of sleeping with Potiphar's wife.

> *"And it came to pass, when his master heard the words of his wife, which she spake unto him, saying, After this manner did thy servant to me: that his wrath was kindled.*
>
> *And Joseph's master took him and put him into the prison, a place where the king's prisoners were bound: and he was there in the prison."*
>
> *– Genesis 39:19-20.*

The prison was another chapter; another phase in the life of Joseph. Joseph was going from one chapter to another. Destiny is like a book with lines, pages and chapters. You keep going from one line to another; from one page to another; from one chapter to another. Until you get to end of your book of destiny where like Paul the Apostle, you cannot confidently declare that you have finished your course.

> *"I have fought a good fight. I have finished my course, I have kept the faith.*
>
> *Henceforth there is laid up for me a crown of righteousness, which the Lord, the righteous judge shall give me at that day: and not to me only, but unto all them also that love his appearing."*
>
> *– II Timothy 4:7-8.*

In prison, Joseph was kept together with the king's prisoners-men who served in very close ranks to the king of Egypt. In the course of time, Joseph became connected to the release of one of the king's prisoners-the butler, by interpreting the dream the butler had.

When Pharaoh now had his own dreams and no one could interpret the dreams of Pharaoh, Joseph through the recommendation of the butler was sent for by Pharaoh. Joseph's encounter with Pharaoh brought in the final push for his destiny. Joseph had come a long way to fulfill his destiny and the final key to the manifestation of his destiny was in Pharaoh having two dreams that no one could interpret. And so in Pharaoh's dreams came the reality of Joseph's destiny.

NO COINCIDENCE WITH DESTINY

Looking at the chronicles of Joseph's life, there were no coincidences. Pharaoh's dreams were because of Joseph's destiny. Pharaoh had a dream so that the destiny of Joseph could become a reality. It was the divine revelation Pharaoh had that brought about the immense wealth of Egypt.

But the divine revelations Pharaoh had were not just because of Pharaoh. The divine revelations that brought about the wealth of Egypt came to Pharaoh because of the destiny of Joseph. The destiny of Joseph was the reason why the revelations of Pharaoh came.

This goes to show that if the revelations that Pharaoh had were as a result of the destiny of Joseph and the wealth of Egypt as a result of the revelations of Pharaoh, then the wealth of Egypt came as a result of the destiny of Joseph. And so destiny is the force behind wealth.

YOUR WEALTH LIES IN YOUR DESTINY

Nothing determines your wealth like your destiny. Nothing gives you access to wealth like destiny. Your wealth is in your destiny. Your wealth is a product of your destiny. Your destiny is the access to your wealth. Your destiny is the key to your destiny. Wealth is totally impossible without destiny. Outside destiny, wealth remains impossible.

Your destiny is the means to your wealth. Your destiny is the route to your wealth. It takes destiny to command wealth. Wealth answers to destiny. Wealth flows through destiny. Your access to your wealth is in your access to your destiny. Until you locate your destiny, you cannot locate your wealth. One sure step to your wealth is locating your destiny.

Before God met with Abraham, Abraham was nothing to write home about. Abraham was a mess; a liability. Abraham, though married, was still living with his father at the age of seventy-five. But when God met with Abraham, everything changed for him. When God met Abraham in Genesis 12, Abraham located his destiny. Abraham accessed his destiny in Genesis 12.

"Now the Lord had said unto Abram,
Get thee out of thy country, and from thy
kindred, and from thy father's house, unto a
land that I will show thee.

And I will make of thee a great nation, and I
will bless thee, and make thy name great;
and thou shalt be a blessing:

And I will bless them that bless thee,
and curse him that curseth thee: and in
thee shall all families of the earth be blessed."

– Genesis 12:1-3.

Abraham's first encounter with God as recorded by scriptures opened Abraham up to his destiny. When Abraham met with God, Abraham had an insight; a preview of what he was ordained to be. Genesis 12 opened Abraham up to his destiny. But In Genesis 13, Abraham is recorded as becoming very rich.

> *"And Abram went up out of Egypt,*
> *he and his wife and all that he had,*
> *and Lot with him, into the south.*
>
> *And Abram was very rich*
> *in cattle, silver and in gold."*
>
> *– Genesis 13:1-2.*

In Genesis 12, Abraham located his destiny. In Genesis 13, Abraham located his wealth. In Genesis 12, Abraham accessed his destiny. In Genesis 13, Abraham accessed his wealth. Destiny came before wealth. Destiny was first located before wealth was located. Destiny was first accessed before wealth was accessed.

Wealth is an allocation of destiny. Wealth is an offspring of destiny. Wealth is born out of destiny. For Abraham to become rich, Abraham had to first of all locate his destiny. It is a covenant sequence. Before you can locate your wealth, you must locate your destiny. Before you can access your wealth, you must first access your destiny.

LOCATE YOUR DESTINY

You can't locate wealth before destiny. Your connection with wealth lies in your connection with destiny. You need a sense of destiny to access wealth. Destiny is what will point you to wealth. This is why in your quest for wealth, you really need to locate your destiny.

Destiny always comes before wealth. Destiny takes priority over wealth. Wealth is nothing without destiny. Wealth is useless without destiny. Wealth is irrelevant without destiny.

The wealthiest men in the world today are men of destiny. Those who command ever flowing wealth are those who have taken time to locate their destinies. The richest men in the world today are those who are standing in the place of their destinies. There is a very strong connection between wealth and destiny.

TWO SIDES OF THE SAME COIN

You can't separate wealth from destiny. Wealth and destiny are so grossly interwoven. Wealth and destiny are too connected; they are inseparable. Wealth and destiny are two sides of the same coin. Any man who must be wealthy and continue on the ascend grid to wealth must first of all lay hold of his destiny. Anyone who is interested in wealth must also be interested in destiny.

Anyone who seeks wealth must first of all seek destiny. Anyone who is pursuing wealth must primarily pursue destiny. Pursuing wealth begins with pursuing destiny. Destiny is the mother of wealth. Destiny is the backbone of wealth.

Everyone created by God is created with a destiny. Everyone created by God has a destiny. Everyone created by God carries destiny. You have a destiny.

> *"Before I formed thee in the belly,*
> *I knew thee, and before thou camest*
> *forth out of the womb, I sanctified thee,*
> *and I ordained thee a prophet unto the nations."*
>
> *– Jeremiah 1:5.*

Before God formed you, He knew you and ordained you to be something. God created you to be something. Just as Jeremiah was ordained to be a prophet, you are ordained to be something. You are not created to be anything neither were you created to be everything. You were created to be something.

Locating your destiny lies in locating what you are created to be. Accessing your destiny lies in accessing what you are ordained to be.

Destiny is not anything. Destiny is not everything. Destiny is something. Your destiny is about something. Until you discover what your destiny is about, you have not discovered your destiny. You belong somewhere. Locating where you belong in life is locating your destiny.

THERE IS A PURPOSE

You were not born because two people had sex, even though primarily that is what it seems. Beyond two people sleeping together and having sex which resulted in you being born, beyond that, you were born because you have a destiny to fulfill. You were born because of destiny.

Destiny is the reason why you were born. Destiny is the reason why you are alive. You are a child of destiny. You are an offspring of destiny. There is a divine mandate over your life. Before your life became your own, your life had been tailored to a particular direction.

Locating your direction in life is locating your destiny. Discovering your path in life is discovering your destiny. There is a divine agenda over your life. There is a divine plan over your life. Abraham located his destiny by locating God's plan for his life.

Abraham accessed his destiny by accessing God's plan for his life. God's plan for your life is the key to unlocking your destiny. God's plan for your life is the blueprint of your destiny. Your destiny is the core product of God's plan for your life.

YOUR LIFE HAS A PLAN

Your destiny is the principal function of God's plan for your life. Outside God's plan, destiny is impossible. Behind every destiny is a divine agenda. Behind every destiny is a divine plan. The plan that brought about Abraham's destiny and eventually made Abraham was not Abraham's plans.

Abraham's plans did not make Abraham. God's plans made Abraham. Your destiny is not a product of your plan. Your destiny is a product of God's plan for your life. The blueprint of your life is not in your agenda. Certainly not! The blueprint of your life is in God's agenda for your life. Locating God's plan for your life and following it is your access to destiny.

You have a destiny of greatness. You have a destiny of wealth. But there is a divine plan behind that destiny. Locating God's plan places you in the shoes of destiny. You did not create yourself. You were created by God. And when God created you, He had a plan for you.

YOU DID NOT CREATE YOURSELF

God created you with a plan for you. God did not just create you for the fun of creating you; God created you because He has a plan for you. You were created because there was a plan in place for you. You were created because there was an agenda in place for you. You were created with a plan. You are a product of a plan.

You are not an accident nor are you a mistake. However circumstantial your birth may have been, the fact still remains that you are a deliberate work of a deliberate plan put together by a deliberate God. You were planned for by God before you were born. This is why you were born where you were born; you were born into the family you were born into; you were born into the country you were born and you were born with the gifts you were born with.

All these are not accidents. All these are all the deliberate plans of God. And without that plan, you don't stand a chance in life. You were not born because two people met; you were born because a plan was formed. That plan is the sole reason why you were born.

"Enter ye in the strait gate: for wide is the gate and broad is the way, that leadeth to destruction, and many there be which go in thereat:

Because strait is the gate, and narrow is the way, which leadeth unto life, and few there be that find it."

– Matthew 7:13-14.

Just like the broad and narrow gate with multitudes on one and few on the other, only very few in life are actually on course with their destiny. Only very few have actually accessed God's plan for their lives and destiny. So many people are operating their lives outside their destiny; so many are living their lives outside their destiny.

From the Scriptures, people are referred to as buildings. Every human being is like a building. The life of a man is viewed as a building.

> ***"Know ye not that ye are the temple of God***
> ***and that the Spirit of God dwelleth in you?***
>
> ***If any man defile the temple of God him***
> ***shall God destroy: for the temple of God***
> ***is holy, which temple ye are."***
>
> *– I Corinthians 3:16-17.*

The same way a building goes is the same way life goes. The process of building is also the process of life. This is why building is living and living is building. Understanding how to build is understanding how to live. Living is in building. Behind every building is a plan.

Every building is a product of a plan. Every building has a blueprint. Before the building begins on ground, the building has already been finished on paper. The building you see on ground has already been finished on paper.

FINISHED WORK

Every building is built twice; first on paper and then on ground. Every building was already finished before it began. Your life was already finished before it began. Everything concerning you has been finished before it began. Your life is the beginning of a finished work. Your life is a finished work.

There is nothing about you that has not been finished. Your joy has been finished. Your success has been finished. Your marriage and family has been finished. Your health has been finished. Your wealth and prosperity has been finished. Your life is a finished product.

There is no reason for you not to succeed because your success has already been finished for you before you were born. There is no excuse for you to be poor because your wealth has already been finished for you before you were born. For you to succeed in this life, you must access what has been finished concerning you. For you to be wealthy, you must access the wealth that has been finished concerning you.

BEGIN WITH A DISCOVERY

Just as a building where before it is finished on ground, it is already finished on paper with the finished work on paper called the building plan; in like manner, you were already finished in the plan of God for your life before you were born. God finished everything concerning you in His plan for you before you were born.

You were perfected in the plan of God for your life before you were born. The plan of God for your life carries your finished life. And your destiny is the totality of your finished life. Accessing everything that has been finished and perfected concerning you is accessing God's plan for your life.

Until you access God's plan for your life, your life has not really started. God finished you before He began with you. Whatever has been finished concerning you can only begin when it is discovered. You are to begin what has been finished and for you to begin what has been finished, you need to locate what has been finished for you.

> *"It is the glory of God to conceal a thing: but the honor of kings is to search out a matter."*
>
> *– Proverbs 25:2.*

The things concerning you are essentially hidden. The things concerning your life and destiny are hidden. God's plan for your life is hidden. And anything that is hidden only needs to be discovered. This is why destiny answers to discoveries. Destiny is a product of discoveries. Your access to destiny lies in your personal discoveries.

You need discoveries to locate destiny. You need discoveries to access destiny. Destiny does not jump on men and men don't just jump into destiny. Destiny is by discoveries. Discoveries connects you to destiny. Discoveries opens you up to destiny. This is why your destiny is your responsibility. Discoveries are the keys that unlock destiny.

> *". . . seek and ye shall find . . . "*
>
> *– Matthew 7:7*

Destinies are products of diligent searching. You must have a searching spirit if you must have a life of discoveries. Finding is by searching. Discovery is by seeking. Only seekers get answers.

> *"Either what woman having ten pieces of silver,*
> *if she lose one piece, doth not light a candle,*
> *and sweep the house, and seek diligently till she find it?"*
>
> *– Luke 15:8.*

In searching for her missing pieces of silver, she had to employ the use of light. And light refers to knowledge.

> *"Thy word is a lamp unto my feet*
> *and a light unto my path."*
>
> *– Psalms 119:105.*

Light is knowledge. In her pursuit for a successful search, that woman had to engage the use of knowledge. Without light finding her missing piece of silver would have been difficult and impossible. But light aided her discovery. Nothing makes discovery possible like knowledge.

Nothing opens you up to discoveries like knowledge. Knowledge is the power behind discoveries. Knowledge is your access to discoveries. In your pursuit for discoveries, you need to engage knowledge. Without knowledge, there will be no discoveries. Giving yourself to knowledge is what connects you to discoveries.

JOURNEY TO WEALTH

WEALTH IS FUNDAMENTALLY A PERSONAL CHOICE

BY: JOSHUA GREAT

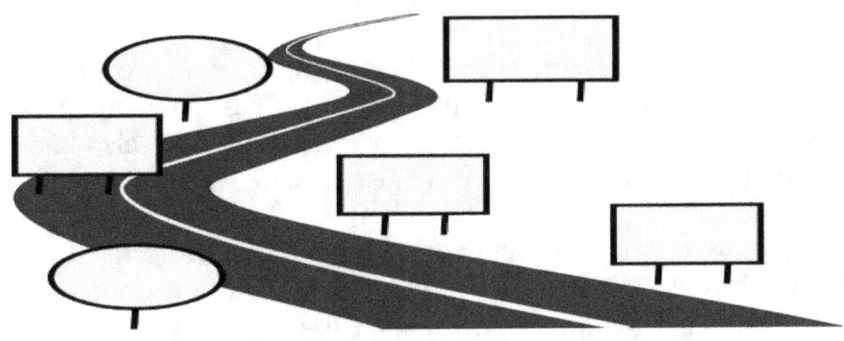

CHAPTER SEVEN
THE STROKE

In the midst of the famine, where everyone and every nation was looking for food, Egypt had food in so much abundance to offer the whole world. And by offering food to the whole world, Egypt became so wealthy.

Your wealth is a product of what you have to offer. Your wealth is in your offering. For you to become wealthy, you must have something to offer. But it is not enough to have something to offer, you must also know how to offer what you have to offer if you must become wealthy.

You must know how to turn what you have into practical gains if you must become wealthy. You must know how to turn your offerings into profits if you must command wealth. What you have to offer must bring you gains.

THE CONVERSION

Just having something to offer does not automatically translate into wealth. Translating what you have to offer into visible profits is your sure access to wealth. Turning what you have into visible gains is your key to wealth. This is why your wealth lies in your ability to make profits from whatever you have to offer.

Your wealth lies in your ability to make gains from what you have to offer. A life of wealth is a life of profits. A life of wealth is a life of increase. Your access to wealth lies in your access to profits. Continuous profit is what brings you into the realms of wealth. When profit becomes continuous, wealth becomes guaranteed. Profits holds the key to wealth.

Every genuine wealth anywhere is a product of profits. Every true wealth is a function of profits and not just profits but continuous profits-steady profits. Wherever you see wealth, you see profits. Wherever you see wealth, you see gains. Wherever you see wealth, you see increase.

In order to overcome the pains of poverty, you need the gains of wealth. A poor man is a man without gains. Poverty is the absence of profits. Your life must be gainful if your life must be prosperous.

THINK PROFITS

Channeling your life towards profits is what puts you on the path to wealth. Gearing your life towards increase is your road-map to wealth. Where there is no gain, there can only be pain. It takes gains to overcome pain. It takes profits to come out of poverty. Poverty bows to profits. If you can make steady profits, you will have no business with poverty.

Loss, pain and decrease are all strongholds of poverty. Your ability to move from pain to gains is what positions you for wealth. Your ability to move from decrease to increase is what gives you access to wealth. Your ability to flow from losses to profits is what opens you up to wealth.

Nothing links you to wealth like increase. Nothing connects you to wealth like profits. The rich are simply masters at making profits. You need to master the wisdom of making profits if you must be rich. People of means are people of profits. Profit is what defines wealth. Profit is what determines wealth. Profit is what brings wealth.

Take a look at Jacob's wealth.

Jacob did not just become rich because he had idea. More importantly, Jacob became rich because he could use his idea to make profits. This is the underlining factor. Having it is not enough; how you use it is what matters. Jacob could translate his idea into practical visible gains. That was the stroke that gave Jacob the break he so desperately needed.

A lot of people have great ideas. A lot of people have great talents and gifts. A lot of people have great possessions and properties. A lot of people have great experiences and all sorts of amazing certifications. A lot of people have so many things but they lack what it takes to turn what they have into visible gains. They lack the genius ability. They lack the genius dimension.

BEYOND OFFERING SOMETHING

It is not what you have that really matters. Rather it is what you do with what you have that actually matters. What you have is nothing if you cannot use what you have. Only very few can profitably use what they have. Only very few can gainfully turn what they have.

Only very few can actually translate what they have into practical visible gains. This is the dividing line between wealth and poverty. This is what separates the rich from the poor. The wisdom of turning what you have into visible gains is the ultimate stroke of wealth. If your idea or whatever you have cannot be translated into visible profits, whatever you have is as bad as nothing. This is where genius is needed.

There is a genius in the pursuit of wealth and the genius of wealth lies in profitably using what you have. The genius of wealth lies in practically translating what you have into visible gains. The genius of wealth lies in turning what is invisible to become visible.

WHERE GENIUS PLAYS OUT

It is pure genius to turn an idea into wealth. It is pure genius to turn a talent or a gift into wealth. It is pure genius to turn an experience or a product into wealth. It is pure genius to turn an opportunity into wealth and the reason it is so is because it is not everyone who can profitably turn things around.

It is not everyone who can translate what they have into visible profits. Genius is not the privilege of everyone even though everyone has in them the capacity of becoming a genius. What is general is not genius. What is common is not genius.

Genius is not common. Genius is not natural. Genius is exclusive. Genius is a privilege; a privilege not tapped by many. A privilege not desired by many. A privilege not coveted or utilized by many. So many prefer the easy life of mediocrity; preferring to remain wretched than to stretch or be stretched.

DESIRE TO BE A GENIUS

The easy life is a mediocre life. The wretched life is a mediocre life. But there is a life greater mediocrity. There is a life beyond mediocrity. It is the genius life. Not too many get to live the genius life. Only very few do. Genius is the privilege of a select few. And you can be among the select few.

You can become a genius. You can strike with a stroke that will amaze your world. There is a genius in you. You can gainfully turn things around. Whatever you have to offer that cannot bring you gain is useless. Whatever you have that is not a plus to you will be useless to you.

The genius of true and enduring wealth lies in turning whatever you have; it could be an idea, an insight, a skill, a talent, an experience, a contact, your beauty, your looks, whatever, into practical visible gains.

Look at Jacob's idea.

> *"And he said, what shall I give thee?*
> *And Jacob said, Thou shalt not give me*
> *anything: if thou wilt do this thing for me,*
> *I will again feed and keep thy flock.*
>
> *I will pass through all thy flock to day,*
> *removing from thence, all the speckled and*
> *spotted cattle, and all the brown cattle among*
> *the sheep, and the spotted and speckled among*
> *the goats: and of such shall be my hire."*
>
> *– Genesis 30:31-32.*

Getting the spotted animals as his portion; looking after Laban's flock and multiplying Laban's flock as well as his own tiny spotted flock of animals was Jacob's idea to Laban. One look at the whole picture shows that Jacob's idea was not a threat in any way to Laban. From Laban's response to Jacob it was obvious that the spotted animals which Jacob took as his portion were greatly disadvantaged in number, looks and size. They were the bad lot.

The spotted animals which represented the few and weak came to Jacob as his own potion while the unspotted animals which were the strong and multitude in number went to Laban. Laban did not see a shift coming. Laban did not see it coming.

SURFACE VERSUS DEPTH

What Laban did not know was that Jacob's idea was not just in taking the spotted animals which represented the weak and the few. No! Far from it! Jacob's idea was in using the unspotted animals which were the strong and multitude for numbers to produce strong spotted animals.

The surface deal of Jacob's idea as Laban understood it was that as the animals multiply accordingly, every spotted animal will go to Jacob and the unspotted to Laban. Since Laban had the strongest and the multitude in his favor, it was expected that as the flocks multiply accordingly, the unspotted will be in the majority for Laban and the spotted in the minority for Jacob.

MAKE IT VISIBLE

Furthermore, since reproduction is not something made by man, there was no way Laban could have argued or questioned Jacob when the scales tilted in favor of Jacob. Jacob had an idea but most importantly, Jacob knew how to translate his idea into visible gains. This was pure genius. Jacob was a genius.

Only a genius could have done what Jacob did. Whatever you have to offer is not enough. Whatever you have to offer is an invisible form of wealth. That invisible form of wealth is not useful in our visible world. Our world needs visibility. Our world relates with visibility.

You can't spend invisible money here. You can't own invisible companies and properties here. What is invisible needs to become visible. Therefore, that invisible form of wealth needs to be translated into a visible form of wealth by making profits. This is where genius plays out.

GO DEEP

Just like Jacob who was a genius, genius does not play out from the surface. Genius plays out from beyond the surface. There is a place beyond the surface; it is called the deep; that is where genius plays out from. Genius plays out from the deep. The capacity of becoming a genius comes from the deep.

The deep is what it takes to become a genius. The deep is the key to unlocking the genius in you. The deep is the secret of all geniuses. All you need to manifest as a genius, is to go deep. Becoming a genius is no small job. Becoming a genius is no child's play. It's no small talk either.

When you become a genius, you become a wonder. You become a mystery. When you become a genius, you see what others can't see. You do what others can't do. You go where others can't go. Your feats and accomplishments become mind blowing; out of this world, if you become a genius. But it comes with a price.

The price of becoming a genius is going deep. The price of becoming a genius is accessing depths. Depth is the place of genius. The deep is where genius is born. If you can go deep, you will emerge a genius. Those who are seen and celebrated as geniuses are all men and women of depths; great depths. Go deep.

THE RICH ARE MASTERS AT THIS

Job was the wealthiest man in his time and age. No one could stand or match the wealth of Job. And yet Job's wealth was not by luck or chance. One of the major secrets to the immense wealth of Job was increase-gains-profits.

When Satan came before God, Job became the issue of discuss between God and Satan. As Satan spoke against Job in trying to discredit Job before God, Satan revealed the key secrets that stood as a major stronghold to the great wealth of Job. And one of those secrets was Job's ability to make profits. Job had a perpetual lifestyle of increase.

*"Then Satan answered the LORD,
and said, Doth Job fear God for nought?*

> *Hast not thou made an edge about him,*
> *and about his house, and about all that*
> *he had on every side? Thou hast*
> *blessed the work of his hands,*
> *and his substance increased in the land."*
>
> *- Job 1:9-10*

Job's wealth was not a gamble nor was it an overnight affair. Job's wealth was a product of continuous increase. Job's wealth was a product of constant profits. Wealth is not a sudden event. Wealth is a journey. Wealth is a process. And the process of wealth is increase. The journey of wealth is profits.

Wealth is principally a journey of continuous profits. You must know how to make continuous increase with your life if you must access wealth. You must master the wisdom of making steady profits. You must imbibe the discipline of gainful living.

More so, making profit is possible. Going from pain to gains is possible. Moving from decrease to habitual increase is possible. Flowing from great losses to unbelievable profits is possible.

Check this story;

> *"He said therefore, A certain noble man*
> *went into a far country to receive for*
> *himself a kingdom and to return.*
>
> *And he called his ten servants, and*
> *delivered them ten pounds and said,*
> *unto them, Occupy till I come.*
>
> *But his citizens hated him, and sent a*
> *message after him, saying,*
> *We will not have this man to reign over us.*

*And it came to pass, that when he was returned,
having received the kingdom,
then he commanded these servants to be
called unto him, to whom he had given
the money, that he might know how much
everyman had gained by trading.*

*Then came the first, saying, Lord,
thy pound had gained ten pounds.*

*And he said unto him, Well,
thou good servant: because thou hast been faithful
in a very little, have thou authority over ten cities.*

*And the second came, saying,
Lord thy pound hath gained five pounds.*

*And He said likewise to him.
Be thou also over five cities.*

*And another came, saying,
Lord, behold, here is thy pound,
which I have kept laid up in a napkin:*

*For I feared thee, because thou art an
austere man: thou takest up that thou layest
not down, and reapest that thou didst not sow.*

*And he said unto him,
Out of thine own mouth will I judge thee,
thou wicked servant. Thou knewest that
I was an austere man, taking up that
I laid not down, and reaping that I did not sow:*

*Wherefore then gavest not thou my
money into the bank, that at my coming
I might have require mine own with usury?*

*And he saith unto them that stood by,
Take from him the pound, and give
it to him that hath ten pounds."*

– Luke 19:12-24.

There are certain secrets to making profits.

1. EXPOSURE

Each of the three servants were given ten pounds, five pounds and one pound respectively. Out of the three servants, two made profits while one made no profit and the reason he made no profit was because he buried what was given to him. He covered what he was given. Burying what he had, robbed him of making any profits.

The first step towards making profits with what you have is uncovering what you have. Expose what you have. What you bury cannot increase. What you bury cannot prosper. What you hide will die. What you cover has no power. Cover kills power. What you cover cannot bring you any profit.

What you hide cannot prosper. You can't bury what you have and expect what you have to bring you profits. Profits begin with exposure. Increase lies in exposure. Until you expose what you have, what you have cannot bring you profits.

MAKE YOUR INCREASE VIA EXPOSURE

Exposure is your key to profits. Exposure is your access to increase. Exposure is what connects you to profits. Increase follows exposure. Increase is tied to exposure. Increase flows in the direction of exposure.

When Solomon became the king of Israel, his only desire was that God would give him wisdom to successfully rule the great nation of Israel. God honored Solomon's desire and gave him wisdom in such a dimension that no other man or king ever had.

*"In Gibeon, the LORD appeared to
Solomon in a dream by night:*

*And God said, Ask what I shall give thee,
And Solomon said . . .*

*Give therefore thy servant an
understanding heart to judge thy people,
that I may discern between good and bad:
for who is able to judge this thy so great a people?*

*And the speech pleased the Lord,
that Solomon had asked this thing,*

*And God said unto him,
Because thou hast asked this thing, and
hast not asked for thyself long life, neither
hast thou asked for riches for thyself, nor
hast asked the life of thine
enemies: but hast asked for thyself
understanding to discern judgment.*

*Behold, I have done according to thy words:
lo, I have given thee a wise and an
understanding heart: so that there was none
like thee before thee, neither after thee shall
any arise like unto thee."*

– I Kings 3:5-6, 9-12.

When God gave Solomon wisdom, nobody was there; nobody knew. Only Solomon knew that God had given him wisdom and yet the wisdom given to Solomon was not just for Solomon but for Israel. The wisdom that was given to Solomon was to enable him govern Israel successfully.

With such wisdom, Israel was to attain unbelievable heights and imperatively become the envy of all nations. Such was the purpose of that which was given to Solomon, king of Israel. Therefore, such a thing given to a man, could not remain hidden or unknown.

TRUTH REQUIRES WISDOM

Solomon had a fundamental responsibility to expose the wisdom that was given to him from God and not cover or bury it if it was to serve its true purpose. Eventually, the wisdom given to Solomon was exposed for all to see in such a manner that aroused so much drama and when people saw what was ultimately exposed, they came in their droves from all the corners of the world for it.

Two harlots each gave birth to a son at the same period and they both stayed in the same place. In the process of time, one of the sons from the two harlots died. The harlot whose child died laid claim to the living child from the other harlot. The two harlots kept arguing over the living child.

Obviously, someone was lying, but how was the one who was lying be undoubtedly revealed or exposed? At a time like this, the truth had to revealed. But for the truth to be revealed, wisdom had to be applied. This was the matter that was brought before Solomon. It was a situation that required wisdom.

WISDOM IS THE ULTIMATE

Truth requires wisdom to be revealed. Truth is not just revealed because it is the truth. Truth must follow wisdom. There are certain truths that if they are not revealed with wisdom, they no longer serve as truths. Just as when the salt loses its savour, they lose their purpose and service.

Truth poorly delivered will be resisted. Truth that is delivered without wisdom will be rejected. Truth is truth. That is true. There is nothing anyone can do about the truth. But truth is lost without wisdom. Wisdom is the ultimate platform for the truth. You don't just say the truth because it's the truth. The truth requires wisdom.

You need wisdom to say the truth. Truth is powerful but only within the context of wisdom. Truth, even though is the truth will lose its purpose and power without wisdom. This was the challenge before Solomon king of Israel. Solomon needed wisdom to reveal the truth.

PROBLEM EXPOSES

The two harlots argued over the living child before Solomon and so telling who the real mother of the child was, looked impossible. But wisdom always has a way with the impossible. The impossible always bows to the force of wisdom.

In handling, this very delicate matter which was before the very eyes of the people of Israel, Solomon demanded that the living child be divided with a sword and shared equally to the two harlots. This was the operational dimension of Solomon's wisdom - the sword.

The harlot who was lying agreed for the child to be divided but the true mother of the child could not stand her for her child to be divided. As such, she cried out and demanded that the child should not be divided but spared and given to the other woman. With this, it became clear who was lying and who was telling the truth.

> *"Then the king answered and said,*
> *Give her the living child, and in no wise*
> *slay it: she is the mother thereof.*
>
> *And all Israel heard of the judgment*
> *which the king had judged: and they feared*
> *the king for they saw that the wisdom of God*
> *was in him to do judgment."*
>
> *– I Kings 3:27-28.*

The first thing that exposed the wisdom of king Solomon was the problem of the two harlots. The first thing that showed that Solomon had something to offer his people and generation was the problem of the two harlots. When the issue of the two harlots came before Solomon, something in Solomon was exposed for people to see. Something great was revealed for many to see.

The problem of the harlots was what exposed the wisdom of Solomon and when the wisdom of Solomon became exposed, multitudes from far and near; kings and nobles; queens and princesses; they all came with their treasures coupled with their substances for the wisdom of Solomon.

> *"And there came of all people to hear
> the wisdom of Solomon, from all kings of the earth,
> which had heard of his wisdom."*
>
> *- 1 Kings 4:34*

Joseph had the ability to interpret dreams. Joseph had the gift of revelation. Supernaturally, Joseph just knew things. Nothing was hard or impossible for Joseph to crack, decode or dissolve. This was wisdom at work. Where others failed, Joseph excelled but there was a twist.

It was in the prison that Joseph's gifts and abilities were exposed. It was in the prison and not in the parlour that Joseph was unveiled. When Joseph was in Potiphar's house, basking in the comfort of his exalted position as the overseer of Potiphar's household, no one knew of Joseph's abilities.

No one knew what Joseph had. No one knew what Joseph carried. No one knew what Joseph was capable of. An untapped treasure was buried in Joseph. Joseph was a veiled wonder waiting to be uncovered.

EXPOSE WHAT YOU HAVE

No one knew the worth and value of Joseph because what he carried inside was buried. But when Joseph crossed over from Potiphar's house to the prison-house; when he crossed over from comfort to problems; when he crossed over from rest to stress, what was buried in him came to the fore. What was hidden was exposed.

More so, it was that exposure that brought Joseph out of prison and placed him in the palace as the second in command to Pharaoh, king of Egypt. Just like Joseph, there is something in you that can change your life. There is something you have that can transform your life. There is something you have that can bring you out of bondage.

There is something you have that can take you to the palace. There is something you have that can make you sit and dine with kings. Its in you.

Its with you. All it needs is exposure. All it needs is an unveiling. Dig it out and expose what you have buried within you.

YOU CAN EXPLODE
If what you have is exposed, your life will explode. If what you carry is unveiled, your life will prevail. If what is with you is uncovered, your life will recover. Your recovery is in your uncovering. There is something to uncover if you must recover. There is something to expose, if you must explode.

So many are suffering simply because what they carry is not exposed. Many are languishing just because what they have is still covered. So many people are not supposed to have any business suffering because of what they carry. So many are not supposed to have any business struggling or being poor and wretched because of what the have.

YOU HAVE SOMETHING
So many are just suffering in vain. So many are just suffering for nothing. There is no need for you to languish in life. There is no need for you to suffer. Your suffering is not necessary.

There is something you have. There is something in you. There is something with you; it could be a gift, an idea, an experience, a contact, a connection, a qualification, a skill, a possession. It could be anything. Everybody has something. No one has nothing. There is no one, no matter how bad or terrible the situation maybe that does not something. You have something.

LEARN FROM THIS WIDOW
There was once a widow who was in so much debt due to her late husband. This poor widow had no practical means of redeeming herself from this quagmire. When her creditors sensed her inability to pay her husband's debts which were now hers, they came to take her sons as payment for what was owed.

To this poor widow, her sons were her only hope and consolation. Her sons were her future. Her sons were her pillars. To take her sons from her was to take her hope and future away. This widow could not afford to have her sons taken from her. This widow could not stand and watch her sons being snatched from her.

THERE IS STILL HOPE

Even though she was poor, she could still do something. Even though she had nothing, she could still act on something. No matter how bad your situation maybe, you can still do something to salvage yourself. There is always something to do.

No situation should make you helpless. You are not helpless. You are not hopeless. There is always hope. In times of seeming hopelessness, you must endeavor to find your hope by all means possible, at any cost. You must find it. It's your duty to find it. You owe it to yourself and dependents to find your hope. It's there, somewhere.

Your hope is your hold. Your hope is your life. If you are hopeless, you are lifeless. It is the core stronghold of your life. This is why to stay hopeless is too risky. It's too dangerous. Hopelessness is a dangerous undertaking.

WHAT DO YOU HAVE

In order to quickly salvage herself and her sons from her terrible impasse, the widow ran to Elisha, the prophet-the only person she felt could help her. Upon her meeting with Elisha the prophet, she narrated her ordeal. After her narration, Elisha asked the widow a very simple question, **what do you have?**

Obviously, whatever the widow had was the master key to the miracle she so desperately needed. Whatever the widow had was the only thing that would change the widow's story and situation for good. There was no other way out.

The widow just had to look for something that she had. Of course when the prophet asked the widow what she had, she was surprised. She must have wondered if Elisha was truly a prophet, the reason being that, if she had something she would have sorted herself out without coming to the prophet. She would not need to meet the prophet.

THERE HAS TO BE SOMETHING

Her coming to meet the prophet was not in any way social but crucial. If Elisha was not mistaken, he would have known as a true prophet should (even though prophets don't know everything and are not supposed to know everything even with their privilege into the prophetic) that she does not have anything.

Therefore, in the confidence of her perceived shallow knowledge, the widow replied the prophet that she does not have anything. Elisha insisted that she must have something without which there is no way out. All of a sudden she remembered that she had a small pot of oil.

" Now there cried a certain woman of the wives of the sons of the prophet unto Elisha the prophet, saying, Thy servant my husband is dead; and thou knowest that thy servant did fear the LORD: and the creditor is come to unto him my two sons to be bondmen.

And Elisha said unto her, What shall I do for thee? tell me, what hast thou in the house? And she said, Thine handmaid hath nothing in the house, save a pot of oil.

Then he said, Go, borrow thee vessels abroad of all thy neighbours, even empty vessels; borrow not a few.

And when thou art come in, thou shalt shut the door upon thee and upon thy sons, and shalt pour out into all those vessels, and thou shalt set aside that which is full.

So she went from him, and shut the door upon her and upon her sons, who brought the vessels to her; and she poured out.

And it came to pass, when the vessels were full,

that she said unto her son, Bring me
yet a vessel. And he said unto her,
There is not a vessel more. And the oil stayed.

Then she came and told the man of God.
And he said, Go, sell the oil, and pay thy debt,
and live thou and thy children of the rest.

- 11 Kings 4:1-7

Unequivocally, the pot of oil was of no real significance to the widow and as such it was not worthy of any mean remembrance. What a pity! Yet it was that insignificant pot of oil that was the key to the miracle the widow so desperately desired. Such is life. What is insignificant is most times the secret behind what is significant.

What is irrelevant is most times the force behind what is relevant. What is unimportant is most times the power behind what seems important. There are so many things that are not relevant and important to so many. Yet those are the things that carry the change that many desperately desire. What a mystery!

There are so many things with so many people that can mysteriously transform their lives but those things are not acknowledged. They are ignored. They are not recognized and the reason is because they seem insignificant. They appear irrelevant. Irrelevance has become the undoing of so many.

IGNORE NOTHING

The perception of irrelevance is one of the major reasons why so many are nowhere today. It is the essential reason behind the regret of so many today. This is why you must be very careful of what you perceive as irrelevant. Be very careful of what you call insignificant. Be very careful of what you conclude as unimportant.

Perception is relative. But the relativity of perception should be objective and productive. This is the accord you owe yourself. There are so many supposed insignificant and irrelevant things within you that can dramatically change your life and story forever. All you need to do is recognize and expose them. Just like the widow, there is something you have; there is something with you and what is with you is the key to your change.

What you have is what will transform your life. All you need to do is to expose what you have. Uncover what you carry. If you can expose what you have, you can be sure of a change in your life. And nothing gives you the opportunity to expose what you have like problems.

PROBLEMS ARE OPPORTUNITIES

Problems are opportunities for exposure. Challenges gives you a platform for exposure. Problems are the forces of exposure. Challenges are the agents of exposure. Most times, what you have will not be exposed without certain challenges. As such, certain problems force certain things within you to come out.

Through the situation of the two harlots, which was a huge challenge to Solomon, the king, the whole of Israel was able to see the wisdom of God in Solomon. The wisdom in Solomon was exposed for all to see. And with this exposure, news of Solomon's wisdom traveled far and wide.

As the news traveled, people came in their numbers from every corner to hear the wisdom of Solomon. People from everywhere, especially from very far and distant lands came to listen to the wisdom of Solomon.

> *"And there came of all people to hear the wisdom of Solomon, from all kings of the earth, which had heard of his wisdom."*
>
> *– I Kings 4:34.*

Among the people who came from far to hear the wisdom of Solomon was the queen of Sheba.

> *"And when the queen of Sheba heard of the fame of Solomon concerning the name of the LORD, she came to prove him with hard questions."*

– I Kings 10:1.

The queen of Sheba came all the way from her country which was a very far distant land to hear and to see for herself the wisdom of Solomon. And the only reason why she came from such distance to hear from Solomon was because she heard of Solomon. The news of Solomon's wisdom had reached her and even went beyond the borders of her country.

BE HEARD AND SEEN

The queen of Sheba had never known or met Solomon before. But despite the fact that she had never met Solomon, she came all the same from such a very far country to meet with Solomon just because of the things she heard about Solomon. If the queen of Sheba had not heard of Solomon, perhaps her path and that of Solomon would never have crossed. But she heard and she came.

People will never come until they hear. People will come when they hear. Until people hear about what you have, people will never come for what you have. Until people see what you have, people will never come for what you have. Exposure is simply making people see what you have.

Exposure is simply making people hear what you have. People must know what you have if they must come for what you have. News of what you have must travel as far as possible into the knowledge of people if people must travel from as far as possible for the sake of what you have.

During the famine, people came to buy from Egypt because they saw and they heard that there was food in Egypt.

> *"Now when Jacob saw that there was corn in Egypt, Jacob said unto his sons, Why do ye look one upon another?*
>
> *And he said, Behold, I have heard that there is corn in Egypt: get you down thither, and buy for us from thence; that we may live, and not die.*

> *And Joseph's ten brethren*
> *went down to buy corn in Egypt."*

– Genesis 42:1-3.

It was when Jacob heard that Egypt had food-it was only then that Jacob moved his sons to go to Egypt and buy food for the family. There are people who need what you have but if they don't know about what you have they won't come for what you have. People will never move towards you until they see something in you.

During the famine, everyone from everywhere came to buy food from Egypt.

> *"And the famine over all the face of the earth:*
> *and Joseph opened all the store houses,*
> *and sold unto the Egyptians: and the famine*
> *waxed sore in the land of Egypt.*
>
> *And all countries came into Egypt to Joseph for to buy*
> *corn; because that the famine was so sore in all lands."*

– Genesis 41:56-57.

You can imagine the quantity and the dimension of food Egypt had to be able to feed the whole world for seven years that the famine lasted. The quantity and dimension of food required to feed the whole world for seven years was unthinkable and unimaginable. And yet Egypt fed the whole world for seven years without complaining even for once.

If Egypt with all her food had covered instead of exposing all her food, nobody would know and nobody would come for Egypt's food; the whole food would have been a huge waste. It does not matter the dimensions of what you have; if nobody knows about what you have, nobody will come for what you have. Whatever you have is nothing if nobody knows about what you have. If nobody knows about what you have, what you have is a waste.

POSITION WHAT YOU HAVE

A lot of ideas are wasting away. A lot of talents are wasting away. A lot of insights are wasting away. A lot of skills are wasting away. A lot of experiences are wasting away. A lot of ministries are wasting away-all because people don't know about them. People don't have any knowledge of what they have.

It is your sole duty and responsibility to bring what you have to the knowledge of people. When people are ignorant of what you carry, what you carry becomes a waste. So many things are wasting away just because people don't know about them.

Anything that is wasting away is wasting away because people don't know about it. Whatever you have to offer that people don't know about is useless. Until people know about what you have to offer, what you have to offer cannot be useful.

MOVE THE WORLD

Use comes with knowledge. Waste comes with ignorance. Ignorance is the mother of waste. Ignorance is the force behind waste. Ignorance is what generates waste. If you feel or think you are wasting away then it is because of ignorance. At the root of every form of waste is the deadly force of ignorance. You need knowledge. You need insight.

People came to hear the wisdom of Solomon because they heard of the wisdom of Solomon. People came to buy food from Egypt because they heard that there was food in Egypt. People came because people heard. Many will only come when many hears and few will only come when few hears. The more people hear about what you have, the more people will come for what you have.

GIVE IT ALL IT TAKES

The level of exposure you give to what you have to offer is what ultimately determines the volume of people that will be drawn to what you have to offer. Exposure attracts people. Exposure draws people. Give what you have, all the exposure you can give to it, so that as much as possible, all people can be drawn from all corners to what you have.

The greatest limitation to every product, every skill, every idea, every experience, and every talent lies in its level of exposure. What you have cannot go beyond its level of exposure. You must always push the boundaries of your exposure. You must continually extend the limits of your exposure.

You must incessantly stretch the confines of your exposure. You must go beyond your level of exposure. There is a need for you to seek out new means to greater exposure.

When the queen of Sheba came all the way from her country to listen to the wisdom of Solomon, she came with all sorts of treasures.

> *" And she came to Jerusalem*
> *with a very great train, with camels that bare*
> *spices, and very much gold, and precious stones . . . "*
>
> *– I Kings 10:2.*

> *"And she gave to the king an hundred*
> *and twenty talents of gold, and of spices,*
> *very great store, and precious stones;*
> *there came no more such*
> *abundance of spices as these which the*
> *queen of Sheba gave to king Solomon."*
>
> *– I Kings 10:10.*

Everything that the queen of Sheba brought with her to Jerusalem, she gave to King Solomon. Everything that the queen of Sheba brought with her to Jerusalem ended as gains and profits to Solomon king of Israel. But if the queen of Sheba did not come to Jerusalem, she would not have brought anything to Jerusalem.

More so, if she had not heard of the wisdom of Solomon, she would not have come to Jerusalem to see King Solomon. Therefore, the profits that came to Solomon from the queen Sheba were as a result of what the queen of Sheba heard of the wisdom of Solomon.

PEOPLE MUST KNOW

Every profit that comes to you is a product of what people hear about you. Every increase that comes to you is a result of what people hear about what you have to offer. Until people begin to hear about what you have, what you have will not command increase from people. The profit that holds the key to your destiny lies with people and until people hear and see what you carry, your profits in the hands of people will remain in the hands of people instead of coming to your hands.

Increase begins with people knowing what you have. Profit begins with people knowing what you carry. Profits lies in people being informed about your ideas, product, experiences, insights, talents, gifts, etc. Get people informed about what you have.

2. TRADE

Out of the three servants who were given treasures, two were profitable while one was unprofitable and the major reason why the servants who were profitable were able to make profits was because they traded. Their profits came by trading.

> *"And it came to pass, that when he was returned, having received the kingdom, then he commanded these servants to be called unto him, to whom he had given money, that he might know how much every man had gained by trading."*
>
> *– Luke 19:15.*

Profits gives you access to wealth and trading gives you access to profits. Anyone who is wealthy anywhere is principally a trader, maybe not in the traditional sense of trading that most people are used to, but in an essential manner. Wealth is basically a product of trading; where you must give something to get something.

This is the platform on which wealth is basically accessed. This is the key element in your journey to wealth. This is why wealth is business. You must have a business mindset if you must become wealthy. Without a business mindset, you cannot become wealthy. Business is the order of wealth.

THE FORCE BEHIND

Trading was the secret behind the profits of the two profitable servants. Trading was also the secret behind the profits of Egypt in the days of Joseph. Profits don't come by luck. Profits don't come by chance. Profits are products of trading. Trading is your key to profits. Trading is what opens you up to profits.

Trading is your channel to profits. Profits answer to trading. Something must go for something to come. But anyone who must enjoy profits must necessarily engage in trading. Anyone who must have profits must become a trader. Trading is a must if profit is your choice. Only traders become gainers. And only gainers become wealthy.

Life is a very big market. The whole world is a very large market where nothing is free. Nothing goes for nothing. If you have nothing to offer, you will continue to suffer. If you have nothing to offer, you stand no chance to prosper. If you have nothing to offer to anyone, no one will offer anything to you.

Whatsoever you will have is a product of what you are ready to offer. If you must gain wealth then you must have something to offer. If wealth must become your profit then you must have something to offer. You must trade something if you must gain something. Nothing goes for nothing.

DETERMINE YOUR OUTPUT

Life rewards you according to your input. It takes something to get something. Everyone you see who has something or anything has given out something to get those things you see with them. Everyone you see who has wealth is giving something to get the wealth you see.

Until you are prepared to give something, you are not prepared to receive something. Only a fool will expect to have something when he has not given anything. Only those who give something, get something. This is what trading is all about.

Trading is not just buying and selling. That is the traditional sense of trading. That is the superficial sense of trading. Trading is beyond buying and selling. Trading is beyond money. Trading is giving what you have to get what you seek. Trading is exchanging and exchanging is changing what you have with someone else for something else.

THE BUSINESS OF WEALTH

Exchange has to do with change. Change is the major character of exchange. Change is the core proof of exchange. Exchange is not possible without change. If there is no change, then there was never an exchange and so changing what you have with something else is what exchange is all about. This is the major thing about trading which in all essence is all about exchanging and locating the people who really need what you have to offer.

Profits come by trading and trading is all about exchanging what you have to get what you seek and in exchanging what you have, you must locate the people who seek what you have to offer or else trading will be impossible. This is why the first rule about trading is discovering your market.

THERE IS A MARKET FOR YOU

The fundamental law of trading is locating your market. The major challenge of business is locating the market. The major success of any business lies in locating the market. Once the market is located, the business will succeed.

It is not enough to have something to offer. More important than having something to offer, is locating the market for what you have to offer. Your market is the heart of your business. Your market is the life of your business. You are not in business because you have something to offer. No! It does not work that way.

Rather you are in business because you have a market for what you have to offer. The market is what brings business. It is the market that puts you in business and not just the product. The product is useless without the market. Until there is a market, there is no business.

You can be so busy and yet not be in business. So many are like that. They are so busy but the sorry truth is, they are not in business. They may appear to be in business because they are so busy but they are not in business. Business is not just about being busy. Beyond being so busy, business is about markets. Being busy does not necessarily put you in business. What puts you in business is your market.

BEYOND STRUCTURES

It is the market that determines business. Without your market, you are not in business. That is why, in business, your market is your essential priority. There are so many people who have wonderful things to offer but because they are yet to get a market for what they have, they can't do business with what they have.

Your market is your business and your business is in your market. Your market is the key to your business. Your market is not the structure or building where people go to buy or sell things; that is the surface thought of what a market is. You must think outside the box. You must go beyond the lines. Glide beyond tradition and sentiments.

If you are after buildings, you will miss your market. If you are after structures, you will not locate your market. Your market is beyond structures and buildings. Your markets are the people who really need what you have. Your markets are those who seek what you carry. Your markets are people and not buildings.

Until you locate your market, you cannot locate your profit. Until you locate your market you cannot locate your wealth. Your wealth is in your market. Your prosperity is in your market. Your success is in your market. Stop wasting your time, energy and resources on people who don't need or appreciate what you have to offer.

MARKET AND WEALTH

Stop wasting your time on people who don't constitute your market force. Stop wasting your energy and resources on people who are not within the scope of your market target. They are not relevant to you. They are not relevant to your wealth. They are not relevant to your destiny. Instead look for those who need what you have to offer and stay with them.

Your market is your treasure. Your market is your gold mine. Your market is your asset. Your market is your fortune. Your market is your wealth. Everyone who has anything to offer has a market for whatever they have to offer. There is a market for everything. There is a market for anything.

There is a market for your ideas. There is a market for your insight. There is a market for your talent. There is a market for your skills. There is a market for your invention. There is a market for your experience. There is a market for your product. There is a market for your calling. There is a market for your ministry. There is a market for your anointing. There is a market for anything.

THE MARKET TREND

The market never comes to meet anyone. Everyone goes to meet the market. Stop waiting for your market to come to you. Stop waiting for your market to arrive. If you are waiting for your market, your market may never come. Stop waiting for people to come and meet you. You need to go and locate your market.

You need to go and locate the people who need what you have to offer. You need to rummage your market. You need to discover your market. The fundamental challenge of business is locating the market. Locating your market is locating your wealth. Discovering your market is accessing your wealth.

It is not enough to have something to offer; you must go a step further to locate the market that needs what you have to offer. This is one of the greatest challenge to wealth. Locating the people who needs what you have is the dividing line between remaining as you are and becoming what you desire.

GO FOR YOUR MARKET

It is the divide between riches and beggary. It is the step between wealth and penury. Everybody may not need what you have to offer, but there are people who definitely need what you have to offer. Locating those who really need what you have to offer is the key to unlocking your wealth.

There is a market for you; go and find it. Go and nose it out. Discover your market. When you discover your market, you will make your mark. When you discover your market, you have discovered your wealth.

JOURNEY TO WEALTH

WEALTH IS FUNDAMENTALLY A PERSONAL CHOICE

BY: JOSHUA GREAT

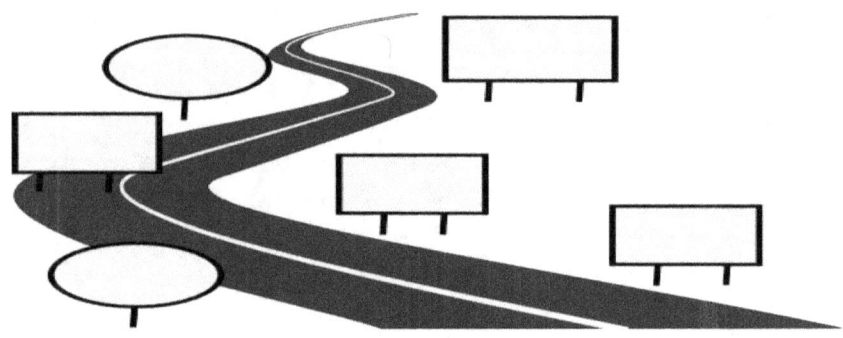

CHAPTER EIGHT
THE FACTOR

It was the food Egypt had to offer during the famine that gave Egypt immense wealth. While everybody was looking for food, Egypt had food in abundance. But the secret to the wealth of Egypt was not just in having food or something to offer. Beyond having something to offer, Egypt knew **_when_** to offer what they had to offer.

The key thing about wealth is knowing *'when'*. Knowing *'when'* is your unhindered access to wealth.

The interpretation of Pharaoh's dream revealed that Egypt had seven years of abundance to prepare for a global famine of seven years.

> *"And in the seven years plenteous years the earth brought forth by handfuls.*
>
> *And he gathered up all the food of the seven years, which were in the land of Egypt; and laid up the food in the cities: the food of the field, which was round about every city, laid he up in the same.*
>
> *And Joseph gathered corn as the sand of the sea; very much, until he left numbering: for it was without number."*
>
> *– Genesis 41:47-49.*

For seven years Egypt kept gathering food against the season of famine. They kept gathering food. But it was until the famine came before they opened their store houses to release what they had.

> *"And the famine was over all the face of the earth: and Joseph opened all the store houses . . ."*

– Genesis 41:56.

It was when the famine came that Egypt opened the stores houses and not before. It was during the famine that Egypt released food to the world and not before. Even when Egypt had gathered so much food in abundance so much so that they lost count, Egypt under the leadership of Joseph still did not open their store houses to the world. They had to wait for a certain time. They had to wait for a particular season to release what they had to the world.

If Joseph had opened the store houses of Egypt thereby releasing food before the famine came, nobody would be interested in what they had to offer. The whole food would have been useless and the reason would have been because everybody already had more than enough food.

TIMING IS EVERYTHING

Scarcity creates relevance and relevance creates wealth. Wealth is more about timing than it is about working or running. Wealth is more about knowing when as it is about doing what. Knowing when to strike; when to wait; when to move; when to withdraw; when to lay low; wealth is more about knowing when.

Wealth is more about working with time. A lot of people have destroyed all their chances in life all because they did not understand the order of proper tîming. Many acted too soon. Many acted too late. Many never acted at all. Many released when they should have withheld and many withheld when they should have released.

The *'when'* factor is the real factor. The *'when'* factor is the wealth factor. Without knowing when, wealth is inaccessible. Without knowing when, wealth is impossible. This is the sole mystery and puzzle governing the whole process and delivery of wealth into the life of anyone.

Anyone who must access wealth, must know *'when'*. Such a person will not be hasty, sentimental or emotional. Such a person will not move or act anyhow because such a person knows *'when'*. More so, because such a person knows *'when'*, such a person will definitely wait for *'when'* because the *'when'* will surely come.

YOU NEED TO KNOW WHEN

Many do not know when; when to step in and when to step out. They do not know when to wait and when to act. Many do not know when to hold and when to let go. They do not know when to bow out and when to stand tall. They do not know when to talk and when to be silent.

Many do not know and because they do not know, they suffer because they do not know. This is the bizarre plague of many. They do not know when. Many do not connect with time. They are out of order and as such they pay the price of ignorance by suffering.

Ignorance has its consequences and punishments. Many are suffering because they are out of order with the seasons of life. Always remember that seasons are the reasons for living.

CONNECTING WITH TIME

Wealth is not just about knowing what to do. Beyond knowing what to do, wealth is about knowing when to do what. Many are so engrossed with what to do but beyond what to do, there is when to do what. Knowing when to do what is what really matters because knowing when to do what is what actually gives you what you desire.

Timing is the missing link in the life of many. Timing is winning. Timing, more than any other thing is what determines winning. If you must win, then you must understand the mysterious order of right timing. If you must rise then you need an insight into the force of proper timing. Greatness can be destroyed all because of wrong timing.

THE WHOLE ESSENCE

Success can be terminated all because of wrong timing. The future can be annulled all because of wrong timing. All that has been built can be destroyed because of wrong timing. All that has been gathered can scattered because of wrong timing. All that is, can be brought to nothing because of wrong timing.

Nothing is relevant without time, Nothing is useful without time. Nothing is possible without time. Understanding that certain things must be done at certain times irrespective of convenience or inconvenience to produce certain results is the cornerstone of all of life's glory. And this is the whole essence and relevance of life.

Time is the whole essence of life. Time is the relevance of life. Without time, life is irrelevant. As such for you to become relevant in life, you must connect with time. Connecting with time is what makes you relevant in life.

IT COMES BY SEASONS

A lot of people have made their lives useless because they were ignorant of time. Being insensitive to time is the undoing of so many people. You can't separate success from time. You can't separate destiny from time. You can't separate wealth from time.

Time is what determines wealth. Time is what programs wealth. Time is what connects you to wealth. Wealth is not about having what to offer and just offering it; beyond that, wealth is knowing when to keep what you have and when to offer what you have.

Wealth is about being smart and smartness is about timing. Knowing what to do, how to do it and when to do it-this is what being smart is all about. Wealth is in knowing *'when'*. Without knowing *'when'*, you will waste. Without knowing *'when'*, what you have is useless.

Without knowing *'when,'* what you have to offer has no relevance. Knowing *'when'* is what gives you wealth. Knowing *'when'* is what makes you or breaks you. Your wealth lies in knowing *'when' to* offer and *'when'* to cover.

There is a time for everything. There is a season for everything in life. Everything has its time including wealth and everyone has their time including you.

"To everything there is a season,
and a time to every purpose under the heaven:

A time to be born, and a time to die; a time to plant; and a time to pluck up that which is planted."
– Ecc 3:1-2.

There is a time for your wealth. There is a time for your success. There is a time for your rising. There is a time for your destiny. Every time is no time and anytime is no time. Your time is not every time. Your time is not anytime. Everyone has his time. My time is not your time and your time is not my time.

There is a time for you and until your time comes, nothing will happen no matter how hard you try to make it happen. Until your time comes, you must wait. Wait for your time. Your time is worth waiting for because everything about you is determined by your time. Everything about you is tied to your time.

Time is what determines everything and everything is determined by time. Everything in life is tied to time. Nothing in life can escape the grip of time. No one in life can break out of the reality of time. Time rules over all.

Everyone and everything in life is controlled by time. Time is the force of life. Time is the rhythm of life. Time is the reality of life. Time is the wisdom of life. In fact, time is life and life is time. Both are so connected and intertwined so much so that they cannot be separated. Time is everything.

BECOME RELEVANT WITH TIME

As you deal with life, you must walk with time. If you must enjoy life then you must understand time. Anyone who must become anything in life must look out for time. Everything in life is hooked to time. Time is the hook of life. There is nothing in life that is without time.

If a woman who is five months pregnant decides to go to the hospital to give birth, she will be turned back; she will be disappointed and the reason why she will be disappointed is simply because it's not yet time for her to give birth. Nothing ever works out until the time for it to work out comes. It does not matter how hard you try, until it is time, every effort is in vain.

It is not just efforts that matters in your quest for wealth, it is timely efforts. It is time-determined efforts that really matters and counts. You don't grow in one day. Growth takes time. Time is what delivers wealth. Time is what delivers success. Time is what delivers destiny.

NOT AS IT SEEMS

So many people are like the woman who is five months pregnant and wants to put to bed but ends up disappointed. So many, in their quest for wealth have ended up so disappointed and frustrated. Disappointments are most times not necessarily bad or satanic. Most times disappointments are the silent signals for wrong timing.

As painful as disappointments maybe, they are most times pointers to the fact that the time is not yet ripe. The time is not right. When the time is not right, disappointment is always the proof. Most times, disappointment is God's way of telling you that it is not yet time.

Most times when disappointments come your way, it is not that you are actually disappointed *per se*, it is just that it is not yet time. Look beyond the disappointments. Stop struggling with time. Stop fighting with time. Stop swimming against the tides of time.

UNDERSTAND THE SIGNS AND SIGNALS

As you make your journey to wealth and destiny, there are signs and signals that will tell you if the time is right or wrong. For sure when the time is not right, disappointments will speak. This is why, one sure thing that silences disappointments is right timing.

The woman with her five months pregnancy who wants to give birth but got disappointed was actually saved. If she had gone ahead, she would have lost her pregnancy and her life would have been in danger. That disappointment saved the woman. That woman may cry, she may complain but her temporary unhappiness is far better than her permanent destruction.

Most times, disappointments save us from destruction. It is very important to note that it is not every disappointment that is actually a sign of wrong timing. It's just that most disappointments are signs that something is wrong, particularly time.

FORCE IS A SIGNAL

Another sign that shows wrong timing is force-lack of ease. When a fruit is not ripe, plucking it is always by force. The right time to pluck a fruit from a tree is when the fruit is ripe. Plucking a fruit when it is not ripe simply means it is not time for the fruit to be plucked.

Whatever you force to happen only shows that the time is not right for it to happen. Whatever you do by force shows that the time is wrong. When the time is wrong, things will be by force. Force is a sign of wrong timing. Ease is the sign of right timing. If the time is right, ease will be the proof.

Joseph while in prison over a false accusation, met with the king's prisoners. In the process of time, one was eventually released-the butler. Knowing that the butler was going to be with the king, Joseph asked the butler to remember him and make mention of him to Pharaoh. But the butler forgot Joseph.

"Yet within three days shall
Pharaoh lift up thine head, and restore
thee unto thy place: and thou shalt deliver
Pharaoh's cup into his hand, after
the former manner when thou wast his butler.

But think on me when
it shall be well with thee, and
shew kindness, I pray thee unto me,
and make mention of me unto
Pharaoh; and bring me out or this house:

For indeed I was stolen away out of
the land of the Hebrews: and here also
have I done nothing that they should
put me into the dungeon."

– Genesis 40:13-15.

Joseph was just being human in trying to work his way out of prison. But it was not yet time for Joseph to leave the prison. It was after two years that Joseph was remembered and brought out of prison before Pharaoh. And the reason why Joseph was brought out of prison was because his time had come.

> *"Then spake the chief butler unto Pharaoh, saying, I do remember my faults this day:*
>
> *Pharaoh was wroth with his servants, and put me in ward in the captain of the guard's house, both me and the chief baker.*
>
> *And we dreamed a dream one night, I and he: we dreamed each man according to the interpretation of his dream.*
>
> *And there was there with us a young man, an Hebrew, servant to the captain of the guard: and we told him, and he interpreted to us our dreams; to each man according to his dream he did interpret.*
>
> *And it came to pass, as he interpreted to us, so it was: me he restored unto mine office, and him he hanged.*
>
> *Then Pharaoh sent and called Joseph, and they brought him hastily out of the dungeon . . . "*
>
> *– Genesis 41:9-14.*

When Joseph's time came, he left the prison without any stress. He left the prison with so much ease. He did not have to beg or lobby to leave. When his time came, everything just worked out. The door that refused to open, opened on its own accord. When your time comes, situations will work in your favor. When your time comes, things will fall into place for your sake.

When your time comes, things will become easy for you. Don't try to force things to happen. Forcing things to happen will only fault things as they try to happen. Force brings faults. Force generates faults. Instead allow things to happen. Flow with the tide of events and be sensitive to the silent signals around you. Just be sensitive. Let your senses come alive.

LEARN TO SENSE THINGS

Learn to sense things that are happening around you. Learn to sense things that are happening to you. Learn to sense things that are about to happen. Just like the eagle who senses the quail prompts of the wind and soars with it even though it maybe opposing, you must learn to sense winds most especially opposing winds.

You must learn to sense and position yourself for opposition even before they take shape. By sensing oppositions, you position yourself to use oppositions to your advantage. By sensing oppositions, you position yourself to flow with oppositions. By sensing oppositions, you position yourself to bend oppositions to your will.

FLOW WITH EASE

Allow oppositions to make you soar to heights unimagined. Don't try to force things to happen just because things are not going your way. Things will not always go your way. Things will not always go as you planned. Life does not always go as planned.

No battle ever goes as planned. The key is not just to plan. Rather the key is to keep planning, As you go with life, you will encounter things you never thought or envisaged. As such, you must keep your plans as fluid as possible. Don't get stuck with your plans.

Your plan must never be final. No! Rather your plans must be fluid; subject to change at any moment. Your plans must be able at any point to accommodate change. Your plans must be able to accommodate the contrary. Despite the contrary, you must learn to bend and not break.

This is the secret of all success and greatness. The gurus of this world understand this principle; the principle of bending without breaking. Bending without blending. When things are not going your way, use whatever comes your way to make a way. Use your oppositions to gain positions. Use your pain to get gain. But don't use force. Use ease. You are not disadvantaged.

Many may think they are disadvantaged but they are not. Their supposed disadvantage is actually their advantage. Their so called loss is actually a plus. But they need ease and not force to do the math.

CARRY ONLY WHAT YOU CAN

Learn how to use ease. Don't carry the whole world on your head. Your head is too small to carry the world. Don't carry what you should not carry. Don't carry what is bigger than you. What is bigger than you will kill you. So many are crushed today because they carried what they should not carry. They carried what was bigger than them.

If you must go very far in this life, you must know what to carry and what not to carry. In this life, so many things will come your way. So many things will beg for your attention. But in all these, you must know what to carry and what not to carry. You must be wise. You must remain firm and focused.

You can't carry everything and you can't carry anything. What you carry matters. What you carry will affect you. It is not everything that comes your way that must become your weight. Always remember that life is a race. There is a race before you. There is a prize ahead of you.

Your life is your race. You can't run the race of your life with weights and loads. Therefore, this is the wisdom of life; stay light and you will go high. Stay light and you will never lack light. Life demands that you stay light.

UNNECESSARY WEIGHTS

You must not be sentimental or emotional about life. Sentiments brings detriments and being emotional makes you lose your motion. So many are bent, their lives are no longer as straight and colorful as it ought to be all because of certain weights. Many are under so many weights.

Heavy weights are pulling many down. These weights are not allowing many to rise or move as they ought to. This ought not be. Learn to be at ease. You may appear to be a fool but you will be glad at the end. Learn the silent principle of ease. Life will be much easier for you if you learn to be at ease.

Your wealth should not be by force. Anything that is by force will surely have faults. There are certain things that are beyond your control. Allow time to arrange certain events and situations in your favor.

THERE ARE WAITING POINTS

Waiting is a must as you journey towards wealth. It is not all about running; there are times when you will have to wait. Knowing when to wait is very crucial and so essential. Wealth is like a puzzle. After working on the pieces and trying to fit in the pieces, sometimes, you just sit back and allow the pieces you have worked on to fall into place by themselves.

There is a time to act and there is a time to watch. Everything has its time. Everyman has his time. You have your own time. This is why it is very important for you to wait for your time. There is a period of waiting in the pursuit of your destiny. There is a waiting season in your quest for wealth. If you don't know when to wait, you won't know how to win.

If you are in a rush, you will only get crushed. If you are in a haste, you will end up as a waste. If you are in a hurry, you will only end up being sorry. Great things are not acquired in a haste. Great things don't come in a hurry. Great things are not gotten in a rush. You must bid your time if you must make your mark. You must wait for your time if you must ever shine in life.

"... he that believeth shall not make haste."

– Isaiah 28:16.

If you truly believe you will get there, you will not be in a haste to get there. Patience is the proof of faith. Patience shows faith. Patience is faith at work. Faith is not just about acting, faith is also about waiting. Waiting is not wasting. Waiting is a form of action. Faith is as much as waiting as it is as much as acting. Anyone who cannot wait has no faith.

Your pursuit for wealth which is a function of your faith must be seen in your patience. Where there is no patience, there is no faith. Impatience is the greatest proof of doubt. Impatience is simply the lack of faith. You can't be full of faith and not be willing to wait. Faith works through patience. Faith puts you at rest.

"That ye be not slothful, but followers of them who through faith and patience inherit the promises."

– Hebrews 6:12.

Faith is totally impossible without patience. He who believes in his time must wait for his time. Waiting is in believing and believing is in waiting. Waiting for your time is believing in your time. When you know and believe that your time will surely come, you will wait for your time. You must believe in your time. You must believe that your time will come. And above all, you must wait for your time.

Check out this story:

"For the kingdom of heaven is like unto a man that is an householder, which went out early in the morning to hire labourers into his vine yard.

And when he had agreed with the labourers for a penny a day, he sent them into his vineyard.

And he went out about the third hour, and saw others standing idle in the market place.

And said unto them; Go ye also into the vineyard, and whatsoever is right, I will give to you. And they went their way.

Again he went out about the sixth

and ninth hour, and did likewise.

And about the eleventh hour, he went, and found others standing idle, and saith unto them, why stand ye all the day idle?

They say unto him, Because no man hath hired us. He saith unto them, Go ye also into the vineyard: and whatever is right, that shall ye receive."

– Matthew 20:1-7.

The master came for the labourers at different times. Some were picked early in the morning; some were picked at the third hour, some at the sixth hour, and some at the eleventh hour. All the labourers were picked. With these different times mentioned, it is very clear that we will not all be blessed at the same time. We will not all become wealthy at the same time. We will not all succeed at the same time.

While some will succeed early, some will succeed later. Everyone will not succeed at the same time. Everyone will not get blessed at the same time. Everyone will not rise at the same time. Whether early or later, the truth is, everyone's rising is guaranteed. Everyone's blessing is guaranteed. Everyone's success is sure. The only difference is time. The only differentiating factor is time.

Time is what makes the difference. Time is what differentiates people. Time is what separates people. The fact that someone else is rising and you are not rising does not mean you will not rise. You will rise when your time comes. Your rising is tied to a time-your time and your time will surely come.

THE DIFFERENCE IS TIME

In Matthew 20, every labourer who wanted to work got hired but they did not get hired at the same time. Listen! Everyone who wants to rise will surely rise. Everyone who wants to succeed will surely succeed. Everyone who wants to be wealthy will surely be wealthy.

As long as there is a desire, nothing is impossible and the reason is because your desire is the driving force of your reality. But be it as it may, everyone will not make it at the same time. Stop measuring your life with others. Stop comparing yourself with others. Their time is not your time. Your time is different from everyone's time.

All the labourers were picked; not even one was left behind. If he came for others he will come for you. If others made it, you will also make it. If others succeeded, you will also succeed. If others became wealthy you will also become wealthy.

Whatever good you see happen to others is surely bound to happen to you. Good is not selective. Good is not exclusive. Good is inclusive. Good is not particular. Good is curricular. Your good will surely come.

NO ROOM FOR ENVY

Let the victory of others become your inspiration. Let the success of others inspire you to your own success. Let the blessings of others become your confidence and motivation. Let the testimony of others assure you of your own testimony. Let the heights of others push you to your own height.

Let the results of others remind you that your own result will come. As their own came, yours will also come. As their own happened, yours will also happen. Let the blessing of others assure you that yours is on the way.

No one under heaven has the singular or primary monopoly of any blessing. No one anywhere under heaven has the power to stop whatever good that has happened to him or her from happening to anyone else. And no blessing under heaven is really particular or exclusive. Every blessing is inclusive.

Whatever good that has happened to anyone anywhere under heaven, is bound to happen anywhere, to anyone under heaven. Whatever you see happen anywhere can happen anywhere. Whatever good that has happened to anyone can happen to you.

Solomon, the great king of Israel said, there is nothing new under the sun. There is nothing that is really particular on its own under the sun.

> *" The thing that hath been,*
> *it is that which shall be; and that*
> *which is done is that which shall be done:*
> *and there is no new thing under the sun. "*

- Ecclesiastes 1:9.

This is wisdom speaking. Life is merely a creative repetition of different forms, shades and orders. Creative repetition is the mysterious order of life. Creative repetition is the core nature of life. As such, inventions and innovations are just creative repetitions. A close look at everything in life, shows that there is always a link; there is always a connection between what was and what is.

There is always a link between the old and the new. There is always a link between the former and the latter. That link is the repetition factor. The new is not an invention by itself. Rather the new is a creative innovation of the old. The new is born out of the old.

NOTHING IS NEW

Nothing is really original on its own. Nothing is really new on its own. Everyone came from someone and everything came from something. The new is not entirely new on its own. The new has parts of the old. There is always part of the old in the supposed new. This is the whole beauty and the quintessential essence of life.

Show me anyone who did not come from someone? Show me anyone who does not have parts or traces of someone in him or her? There is no one. That is why everyone resembles someone in a way because everyone came from someone. We function by resemblance. We exist by resemblance.

Life is by resemblance. And where there is no resemblance, there will be no acceptance. Acceptance comes with resemblance. Acceptance is mainly by resemblance. Can you imagine a black couple giving birth to a white baby? Acceptance will be hard or impossible. Whatever must be accepted must have a resemblance. This is one of the basic functionalities of life and her existence.

Whatever or whoever must exist in this life must resemble something or someone to exist. That is the fundamental order of life. There is no one and there is nothing that can exist on its own, by itself. The fact that its different does not mean its new. Whatever you think is new, came from something; it came from somewhere.

Whatever you think is new, is only a creative repetition of what has been. If it has happened anywhere before, then it will happen again. Life is turn by turn. Everyone has his own turn. When your turn comes, things will surely turn to you. Things will surely turn in your favor if only you can wait for your turn.

> *" I will overturn, overturn,*
> *overturn it: and it shall be no more,*
> *until he come whose*
> *right it is; and I will give it to him. "*
>
> *– Ezekiel 21:27.*

Your turn is coming. There is no need to be in a hurry or get angry at the blessings of others. There is no need to feel bad at the progress of others. There is no need to become bitter or envious of the success of others. You can't be bitter against someone and become better than that person. You can't be bitter and be better. Bitterness destroys better days. Bitterness hinders better days.

Bitterness sucks goodness out of a man. Bitterness dries a man. If you must become better then you must not be bitter. This is why it is a must for you to rejoice with those who rejoice. Celebrate with those who celebrate, bearing in mind that everyone's blessing around you is only an indication that your own will come.

WAIT OR WASTE

If the labourers of the sixth, nineth and most especially the eleventh hour had not waited, they would have missed the master. There are certain things in life that you must definitely wait for. If you miss waiting you will miss it. Certain things don't come in a hurry.

Certain blessings and opportunities don't come in a hurry. Certain things demand that you wait for them. Certain blessings and opportunities demand that you wait for them. You can't journey through life in a hurry. If you are in a hurry, you will miss and lose so many things.

JUST WAIT

You must learn how not to be in a hurry. You must learn how to wait. No one really knew how long those labourers waited especially the eleventh hour labourers. They just kept waiting.

Patience does not count the time nor does it look at the time. Patience only counts on faith. Patience only looks on faith. Patience only believes. Patience never considers how long. Those labourers who waited did not even mind what people will say or think of them while they were waiting at the market place. They just kept waiting.

Patience does not consider what people say. Patience does not consider what people thinks. Patience stands above people. Patience stands above opinions. This is why waiting is not easy. Patience is not an easy virtue.

PRESSED AGAINST MEASURE

With patience comes pressure. The challenge of patience is staying above pressure. You can imagine the pressure over those labourers especially the eleventh hour labourers. It was getting late and the market was closing and yet those labourers kept waiting. It appeared as though the master was not coming for them even though he came.

Pressure will always contend with patience. Pressure is an enemy of patience. If you give in to pressure, you will destroy your patience. Pressure is the force behind impatience. Those who gives in to pressure, cannot be patient. Many can no longer wait not because they don't want to wait but because they are under pressure.

If patience must have his way, you must stay above pressure. This is why patience is for the strong. Patience is tough. Patience is not for the weak neither is patience a sign of weakness.

THE ABILITY IN INABILITY

Patience is a sure sign of strength. Only the strong can wait. It takes strength to wait. Anybody can act but only very few can wait. The lack of patience is simply the lack of strength. Impatience is a major form of weakness. A man's strength is not just in the display of his energy but also in the silence and tenacity of his patience. A man's strength is also in the display of his restraint. Sometimes inaction is far better than action.

Your ability to remain calm in the midst of the storm is great strength. Your ability to refrain no matter the pressure is great strength. Patience is one true measure of a man's strength. Patience is the inner strength of a man. No matter how strong a man thinks he is, if he is not patient he is wrong; he is not strong. Patience is the ability to withstand pressure without losing measure.

THERE ARE THREE MAJOR PRESSURES IN LIFE

THE PRESSURE OF TIME

The labourers of the eleventh hour waited until the master came. Everyday has twenty-four hours. Twelve hours for the day and twelve hours for the night.

Jesus said;

"I must work the works
of him that sent me while it is day.
The night cometh when no man can work."

– John 9:4.

Jesus made it clear that the day is for work and the night is not for work but for rest and so the eleventh hour labourers just had one hour to end the day's work. With the end, they would have missed being hired by the master. But despite the one hour left, the labourers were not discouraged by the time.

They stood their grounds and waited. They did not mind the time. They just kept waiting. Those who mind the time always miss their time. Patience does not mind the time. Patience does not look at the time. Patience only minds hope. Patience only looks at hope. Hope is the focus of patience. Hope is the stronghold of patience.

If you must be patient, then you must be very hopeful. Hope is what makes patience possible. The patient are very hopeful. As long as you are still hopeful, patience will not be hard. It is when hope is gone that patience becomes tough.

HOPE IS THE FOCUS

You must remain hopeful if you must stay patient and one way to remain hopeful is to remove your focus from time. No one can focus on two things. Everyone can only maintain one focus at a time. You can't put your eyes on many things. They will drain you. You must zero your eyes to what really matters and hope is what really matters. You must zero your eyes on hope in order to stay patient.

You can't be waiting and be concerned about time. You can't fix your mind on patience and fix your mind on time. In your patience, you must let go of time. In your patience, you must take your eyes and your focus away from time.

Job, in his trials, while waiting for a turn around from God, boldly declared:

> *"... all the days of my appointed time*
> *will I wait, till my change come."*

– Job 14:14b.

Patience waits till the end. Even when it appeared to be late, the eleventh hour labourers waited. They remained hopeful. The reality of time cannot be ignored. But despite the reality of time, you must hold on to your hope. This is the battle and struggle that surrounds everyone.

Even when it appears to be late, you must still remain hopeful and patient. Patience does not see lateness. Patience does not consider lateness. Even when it appears to be late, patience does not cower into the prevailing reality of lateness. It is this reality that actually cripples patience.

It does not matter what the time says, patience does not consider lateness even in the face of prevailing lateness. Patience believes that no matter how late the time may seem or appear, the time is never late. Patience believes that all things will be just on time.

There is no lateness with patience. You need to bring yourself out of the pressure of time. You need to bring yourself to a level where you are not affected or offended by time no matter how late the time may look or seem. And that can only be by believing that God is never late.

HOW YOU SEE THINGS MATTERS

Lateness is only an appearance shaped by a perception. Lateness is purely a perception. If you see the time as being late then the time will be late but if you see the time as not being late no matter its appearance of lateness, the time will not be late for you.

How you see things matters. How you view issues matters. Everything is perception-perception about your situation and about life. And perception goes beyond seeing. Perception is about having certain insights and forming certain opinions about issues.

Perception is how you see. Your perception is what shapes your reality. Your perception is what determines your reality. There is no lateness with God. God is always on time. You need to believe and hold on to your faith. Patience does not have time.

Patience only has faith. Patience only has hope. Patience does not consider time. Patience only considers faith. Patience does not consider how long? Remove your focus from time and fix your focus on God.

THE PRESSURE OF PEOPLE
Another pressure that tends to affect the patience of many is the pressure of people. People can make you do things you are not supposed to do. People can push you. People can squeeze you. You must learn to stay above the opinions and criticisms of men. You must learn to stay insulated from the seeming and the unseeming pressures of people.

When God promised Abraham a son, God was not joking. God meant it. God was actually going to give Abraham a son but Abraham will have to wait. Abraham waited and was willing to wait for God to give him a son. But after a while, Sarah (Abraham's wife), could no longer wait. And her excuse was that she was growing older.

Sarah approached Abraham because she felt time was no longer on her side. With her age, Sarah reasoned that it will be totally impossible for her to bear children.

*"Now Sarai Abram's wife bare him no
children and she had an handmaid,
an Egyptian, whose name was Hagar.*

*And Sarai said unto Abram,
Behold now, the LORD hath restrained me
from bearing: I pray thee, go in unto my maid;
it may be that I may obtain children by her.
And Abram hearkened to the voice of Sarai.*

*And Sarai Abram's wife, took Hagar her
maid the Egyptian, after Abram hath
dwelt ten years in the land of Canaan,
and gave her to her husband Abram to be his wife."*

– Genesis 16:1-3.

Impatience will always make you do things that you will later regret. Regret is always the result of impatience. Regret is always the end of impatience. If you are impatient, you will regret your impatience. In approaching Abraham, Sarah who by now had given herself to the pressure of time, convinced Abraham to marry Hagar so that Hagar could have children for Abraham and by extension she could call Hagar's children her own children. This was Sarah's way of dealing with her supposed childlessness.

STAY AWAY

On his own, Abraham would not have slept with Hagar. But Sarah pushed Abraham. It was because of Sarah that Abraham slept with Hagar; an act that Sarah really regretted. Stay away from people who remind you of your challenges and situations.

Stay away from those who make it a habit of reminding you of what you are going through. Those kind of people only drain the hopes of people and bring them under the bondage of undue pressure. Stay away from those who remind you of your hopelessness and helplessness. Stay away from those who remind you of your past and mistakes.

Stay away from those who don't see anything good in you. Those who remind you of your problems only bring you under pressure. Don't allow yourself to be pushed by men. Stay with those who encourage and inspire you. Stay with those who believe in you. Stay with those who point you to your blessings and miracles.

THE PRESSURE OF SITUATIONS

The last form of pressure is the pressure of situations. Situations can bring someone under undue pressure. Situations can push people to do things that they ordinarily would not do. Situations can bend people and make them blend with their vomits.

Samuel the prophet told Saul the king of Israel to wait for him at Gilgal for seven days. On the seventh day, he was going to come and perform the sacrifice. This sacrifice was to guarantee Israel's victory in battle and also establish Saul's reign as king over Israel. The important thing about this sacrifice was that this sacrifice was not to be performed by anyone except Samuel the prophet.

> *"And thou shalt go down before me in Gilgal; and behold, I will come down unto thee, to offer burnt offerings, and to sacrifice sacrifices of peace offerings; seven days shalt thou tarry, till I come to thee, and shew thee what thou shalt do."*
>
> *- I Samuel 10:8.*

This was Samuel's clear instruction to Saul. But Saul disobeyed Samuel's instruction because he gave in to the pressure of the situation. When Saul saw his people scattering away from him in battle because the enemy was closing in on him and yet it was the seventh day and Samuel appeared not be coming as promised, Saul could no longer wait again.

Saul, out of impatience, performed the sacrifice-something he should not have done. And that singular act of impatience terminated Saul's reign over Israel. You must not allow yourself to be moved by what you see happening to you and around you. What happens around you is not as important as what happens in you.

HANDLE THE HEAT WITHIN

How you react to what happens around you is far more important than what happens to you. You must learn to see God in every situation and wait for God. Wealth is impossible without patience and patience is a choice.

You can choose to wait or not to wait. You can choose to wait or waste. You can choose to rush and be crushed. You can choose to be hasty or refrain from haste. The choice is yours. At the end, you are a product of your choices.

Whether you will make it or not lies in the choices you make. Whether you will become wealthy or poor; it's your choice; it's up to you. You can choose to be wealthy and begin your journey to wealth.

The choice is yours.

ABOUT THE AUTHOR

Sweeping across the length and breath of our land is a great move causing a deep hunger and thirst for something far higher and greater than motivational talks, vain philosophy, spiritual concoctions and religious slavery. This move seeks to bring to the fore, the cream of what has been as ordained by God for a sure manifestation in these last days.

Called of God with a very clear mandate to TRANSFORM LIVES THROUGH THE HIDDEN WISDOM OF GOD now revealed unto our glory with a three-point mantra-WORD, PRAYER AND DELIVERANCE, JOSHUA GREAT has for close to two decades been part of that move that seeks to birth God's agenda in these last days.

He is the president of JOSHUA GREAT MINISTRIES INTERNATIONAL; an Apostolic ministry with diversified operations in Nigeria. He is also the senior pastor of WORD HABITATION.

As a celebrated author, pastor and teacher, he is happily married to PRAISE. They are blessed with three lovely children.

Author's contact - +2348066948888, +2348035560364
or facebook/joshua greatt.
email - joshuagreatt@gmail.com

ABOUT THE BOOK

WEALTH IS FUNDAMENTALLY A PERSONAL CHOICE. Before wealth can become possible, wealth must first be chosen. You must consciously and deliberately choose wealth if you must enjoy wealth. **WEALTH IS NEVER ACCIDENTAL. WEALTH IS ALWAYS INTENTIONAL. WEALTH IS A CHOICE.**

You can go from mere surviving to mega impact. You can go from just enduring life to really enjoying life. You can go from being in so much debt to super abundance. You can rise and live a life of complete freedom especially financial freedom. You can live you DREAM.

The choice is absolutely yours.

This book, Journey to Wealth, will unquestionably take you on a mysterious trip into the glorious realms of wealth.

- In this book, Journey to Wealth, you will discover -
- The Enemy Called Survival
- The 5 Major Secrets To Overcoming Survival
- The 5 Fundamental Keys That Commands Wealth
- How To Access The Wealth Within
- The 3 Crucial Disciplines Of Wealth
- To Go Beyond The Ordinary
- The Ancient Laws Of Wealth
- How To Uncover Your Wells Of Wealth
- Wealth And Destiny-How They Connect
- The 3 Great Strokes Of Wealth
- The Fundamental Concepts Of Right Timing And Waiting
- How To Handle Pressure
- And So Much More

YOU CANNOT READ THIS BOOK AND REMAIN THE SAME.

This book, Journey to Wealth, will definitely set you on a new path and ultimately transform your life thereby taking you to realms that will surely blow your mind and amaze your world.

Your CHANGE has come!